STEF SMITH

Stef Smith is an multi-award-winning writer working to international acclaim.

Work includes *Enough*, *Girl in the Machine*, *Swallow* (Traverse Theatre); *Nora : A Doll's House* (Glasgow Citizens Theatre/ Young Vic, London); *The Song Project*, *Human Animals* (Royal Court); *Acts of Resistance* (Headlong/Bristol Old Vic); *Love Letter to Europe* (Underbelly); *How to Build a Nation* (Young Vic); *Remote* (National Theatre Connections Festival); *Tea and Symmetry* (BBC Radio); *Smoke (And Mirrors)* (Traverse Theatre & Dot Istanbul for Theatre Uncut); *Back To Back To Back* (Cardboard Citizens); *Cured* (Glasgay! Festival); *Grey Matter* (The Lemon Tree, Aberdeen); *Woman of the Year* (Òran Mór, Glasgow) and *Falling/Flying* (Tron, Glasgow).

Stef has won three Scotsman Fringe First Awards for *Roadkill*, *Swallow* and *Enough*. *Roadkill* also won an Olivier Award for Outstanding Achievement in an Affiliate Theatre, a Herald Angel Award, the Amnesty Freedom of Expression Award, a Fringe First Award, a Total Theatre Award for Innovation, and the Edinburgh International Festival Fringe Prize. *Swallow* opened to widespread critical acclaim, and also won the Scottish Arts Club Theatre Award. *Girl in the Machine* won the 2019 Science and Theatre Drama Award in Germany.

Recently Stef took part in the BBC Drama Writers Room and her Digital Drama Short pilot *FLOAT* was released on BBC iPlayer in October 2019.

Stef is currently under commission to the Lyceum Theatre, Guildhall School of Music & Drama, Leeds Playhouse, National Theatre of Scotland, Royal Exchange Theatre and is on attachment at the National Theatre Studio. She is also an Associate Artist at the Traverse Theatre, Leeds Playhouse and Playwrights' Studio, Scotland.

Stef Smith

NORA : A DOLL'S HOUSE

A radical new version of
Henrik Ibsen's play

NICK HERN BOOKS
London
www.nickhernbooks.co.uk

A Nick Hern Book

Nora : A Doll's House first published as a paperback original in Great Britain in 2019 by Nick Hern Books Limited, The Glasshouse, 49a Goldhawk Road, London W12 8QP

Reprinted in this new edition in 2020

Nora : A Doll's House copyright © 2019, 2020 Stef Smith

Stef Smith has asserted her right to be identified as the author of this work

Cover photograph by Mihaela Bodlovic

Designed and typeset by Nick Hern Books, London
Printed in the UK by Mimeo Ltd, Huntingdon, Cambridgeshire PE29 6XX

A CIP catalogue record for this book is available from the British Library

ISBN 978 1 84842 950 5

Nora : A Doll's House was originally produced by the Citizens Theatre and performed at Tramway, Glasgow, on 15 March 2019, with the following cast:

THOMAS 1/2/3	Tim Barrow
NATHAN 1/2/3	Michael Dylan
NORA 2/CHRISTINE 1	Maryam Hamidi
NORA 1/CHRISTINE 3	Anna Russell-Martin
NORA 3/CHRISTINE 2	Molly Vevers
DANIEL 1/2/3	Daniel Ward

Director	Elizabeth Freestone
Designer	Tom Piper
Lighting Designer	Lee Curran
Composer/Sound Designer	Michael John McCarthy
Movement Director	EJ Boyle
Fight Director	Raymond Short
Associate Lighting Designer	Jason Addison
	(ALD Lumiere Scheme)
Assistant Director	Joanna Bowman

A new production of *Nora : A Doll's House* opened at the Young Vic, London, on 11 February 2020, with the following cast:

NATHAN 1/2/3 — Mark Arends
NORA 2/CHRISTINE 1 — Natalie Klamar
THOMAS 1/2/3 — Luke Norris
NORA 3/CHRISTINE 2 — Amaka Okafor
NORA 1/CHRISTINE 3 — Anna Russell-Martin
DANIEL 1/2/3 — Zephryn Taitte

Director — Elizabeth Freestone
Designer — Tom Piper
Lighting Designer — Lee Curran
Composer & Sound Designer — Michael John McCarthy
Movement Director — EJ Boyle
Fight Director — Kev McCurdy
Casting Director — Sophie Parrott CDG
Jerwood Assistant Director — Júlia Levai
Boris Karloff Trainee Assistant Director — Simonne Mason

Júlia Levai is supported by the Jerwood Assistant Director Program at the Young Vic.

Simonne Mason is supported by the Boris Karloff Trainee Assistant Director Program at the Young Vic.

Young Vic

About the Young Vic

Based on The Cut in London's Waterloo, we produce new plays, classics, musicals, adaptations of books, short films, digital projects and game-changing forms of theatre, attracting large audiences from many different backgrounds. We forge deep connections in our neighbourhood through our **Taking Part** programme, where we engage with over 15,000 people every year via a wide range of projects, from skills-based workshops to on-stage performances. We give 10% of our tickets free to schools and neighbours, irrespective of box-office demand, and we are committed to keeping all ticket prices low.

Our **Directors Program**, the only scheme of its kind, has been running for nearly twenty years and offers young directors a unique opportunity to develop their craft through skills workshops, peer-led projects, paid assistant-directing roles through the **Genesis Fellow**, the **Jerwood Assistant Director Program** and the **Boris Karloff Trainee Assistant Director Program**, as well as access to the **Genesis Directors Network**. Twice a year, the recipient of the **Genesis Future Directors Award** stages a show in The Clare theatre at the Young Vic with full support from the Young Vic's creative, administrative and production teams, enabling us to support and nurture an emerging director as a part of the Young Vic programme.

For many years, the Young Vic has been synonymous with inclusivity, accessibility and creativity. We catalyse debate and channel our work into the digital world, to reach new audiences and continue conversations outside of our four walls. We foster emerging talent and collaborate with some of the world's finest directors, performers and creatives; creating award-winning productions which engage with the world we live in.

Artistic Director: **Kwame Kwei-Armah**
Executive Director: **Despina Tsatsas**

youngvic.org

The Young Vic's Supporters
The Young Vic receives public subsidy from Arts Council England and Lambeth & Southwark Borough Councils.

About the Citizens Theatre

The Citizens Theatre is Glasgow's major producing theatre and one of the leading theatre companies in the UK. Over the last 75 years, the Citizens has built an international reputation for producing innovative shows on stage, alongside a highly regarded learning programme.

The Citizens is led by Executive Director Alex McGowan and Artistic Director Dominic Hill, who is regarded as having 'a talent for classical drama which is genuinely world class' (*Daily Telegraph*). Fondly known as the Citz, the company presents bold new interpretations of classic texts and, uniquely, offers audiences the opportunity to attend performances for as little as 50p.

As its name suggests, the theatre believes in breaking down barriers to engagement with the arts and throughout the year offers a range of opportunities for people of all ages and backgrounds to take part.

The Citizens' beautiful Victorian home in the Gorbals is currently closed while it undergoes a major redevelopment. This will be the first comprehensive, integrated redevelopment of the building in its 140-year history. The project will transform the experiences of audiences, participants and performers and secure the future of one of Scotland's most iconic buildings and theatre companies. During the redevelopment, the theatre continues to present shows in Glasgow and across Scotland.

For the latest information about the Citizens Theatre visit **citz.co.uk**

Acknowledgements

My sincere appreciation to the cast, crew and creatives who were involved in the making of *Nora : A Doll's House*. Both at the Citizens Theatre in Glasgow and the Young Vic in London.

My thanks to Dominic Hill for developing and believing in this play, Frances Poet for her endless support, and as always, my agent Davina Shah and the entire team at Nick Hern Books.

With thanks to my friends who held me up during the making of this play. Especially, Dawn & Ewan, Rose & Jack and Helen & Alan – who without question gave me their homes and hearts. And my family for their endless encouragement, support and stories of the 1960s.

Finally, thank you to Elizabeth Freestone for her care, courage and collaboration.

S.S.

sometimes
the whole world of women
seems a landscape of
red blood and things
that need healing,
the fears all
fears of the flesh;
will it open
or close
will it scar or
keep bleeding
will it live
will it live
will it live and
will he murder it or
marry it.

Lucille Clifton
'she is dreaming'

In a murderous time
        the heart breaks and breaks
                and lives by breaking.
It is necessary to go
        through dark and deeper
                dark and not to turn.

Stanley Kunitz
'The Testing-Tree'

Characters

NORA 1
NORA 2
NORA 3
THOMAS 1
THOMAS 2
THOMAS 3
CHRISTINE 1
CHRISTINE 2
CHRISTINE 3
NATHAN 1
NATHAN 2
NATHAN 3
DANIEL 1
DANIEL 2
DANIEL 3

For the premiere production in the spring of 2019, we used the following doubling:

NORA 1/CHRISTINE 3
NORA 2/CHRISTINE 1
NORA 3/CHRISTINE 2

When the script states NORA (*all*), *all the performers playing Nora should perform those words.*

THOMAS 1/2/3
NATHAN 1/2/3
DANIEL 1/2/3

When the script states THOMAS (*all*), *all the performers* not *playing Nora should perform those words.*

Writer's Note

Any character with a '1' after their name exists in 2018

Any character with a '2' after their name exists in 1968

Any character with a '3' after their name exists in 1918

This play is set in a living room, over three consecutive days in December.

The writer suggests that on stage there are two doors – one leading to the outside world, one leading into the rest of the house. There should be some chairs for people to sit on, there might also be a Christmas tree.

For simplicity and clarity all stage directions refer to the singular, i.e. 'Nora', not 'Noras'. This does not mean the action should not / cannot be performed by all the performers.

A forward slash (/) denotes an interruption.

Where entirely necessary the actors can change words to suit their own dialect.

All and any suggestions to the set, design, movement, entrances and exits are meant merely as helpful guidance. Imagine it as you wish.

This text went to press before the end of rehearsals and so may differ slightly from the play as performed.

DAY ONE

NORA 1

A woman walks into her home. It's warm and welcoming, unlike outside where there is ice on the ground and snow in the air and not far from here a river has slowed down to a standstill. The woman enters her home and her hands and heart thaw. She enters her home and her breath changes from a ghostly swirl to being unnoticeable. She enters her home and there is a particular smell that hits the back of her throat, lavender. A scent that covers the smell of carpets and children and milk and medicine and sweat and sick and shit and sex and sin and... lavender. Years ago, she decided she wanted her whole life to smell of lavender and so, it does. The smell helps keep her calm as she drags in the Christmas tree. It's a little sad looking, a little sullen looking. She haggled the man down to half-price and then gave him a touch more as a tip. Even though she shouldn't have, even though she doesn't have it to spend on a tip, she did. Kindness comes back around, she thought as she dragged the dead-looking spruce through the streets. She dragged it across six crossings with a stack of shopping bags slung over her shoulder and a smile on her face. And the whole time she hummed in a note slightly too high for her voice, so that by the time she was home her throat was burning. Though she quite liked that feeling of fire happening inside of her. It kept her going as she dragged the crumbling

Christmas tree up the stairs to her house.
Bump. Bump. Bump /

NORA 2   A woman walks into her home. It's warm
and welcoming, unlike outside where there
is ice on the ground and snow in the air and
not far from here a river has slowed down to
a standstill. The woman enters her /

NORA 3   A woman walks into her home. It's warm
and welcoming, unlike outside where there
is ice on the ground and snow in the air and
not far from here a river has slowed down
to a /

NORA 2   A woman walks into her home. It's warm
and welcoming /

NORA 1   Unlike outside where there is ice /

NORA 3   On the ground and snow in the /

NORA 1   Lavender. Years ago, she decided she
wanted her whole life to smell of /

NORA 2   Carpets and children and milk and medicine
and /

NORA 3   A crumbling Christmas tree /

NORA 2   A pocket of pills /

NORA 3   A bag of sugar /

NORA 1   A bottle of /

NORA 2   She passed her children playing and she
pretended not to notice.

NORA 3   She passed her children playing and their
laughs were /

NORA 1   Bump. Bump. Bump /

NORA 2   She passed her children playing and /

NORA 1   She passed her children playing and /

NORA 3	The burning inside of her.
NORA 2	That feeling of fire.
NORA 1	A smile on her face.
NORA 2	She thinks of holding her children. That very particular way you hold a child.
NORA 3	That very particular way her husband holds her.
NORA 1	She thinks of holding her children /
NORA 2	She thinks of how her husband holds her /
NORA 3	Panting and praying and sweating and /
NORA 2	Bump. Bump. Bump /
NORA 1	Lavender and lovely /
NORA 3	And sweating and swearing and /
NORA 2	Lovely and loving /
NORA 3	And panting and /
NORA 1	Fuck. She expels on an exhale.

NORA *catches her breath. Studies the tree. Takes off her jacket.*

Fuck.

A moment of silence.

NORA 3	And these three different and distinct lives ripple out and grip and grope at the seams of the other's existence.
NORA 2	Three different and distinct women stand on the edge of each

other's /

NORA 3	A woman stands /
NORA 1	The women stand beside their bags of shopping. And sigh.

NORA *sighs*.

NORA 3	Because it's 1918.
NORA 2	It's 1968.
NORA 1	It's 2018.
NORA 3	And out of her handbag she pulls a bag of sugar.
NORA 2	A little case of pills.
NORA 1	A small bottle of alcohol.
NORA 3	Rations had restricted her diet, so, no matter how much money she had to spend she was only given a single small bag of sugar, and she does have money to spend. Well, her husband has money to spend.
NORA 2	And she might not have too much of anything, but she has plenty of these powdery unpleasant-tasting pills. These little helpers of middle-class mothers.
NORA 1	And it's one of those small bottles of alcohol, that people only buy when they are broke or broken or both. She could only afford a small one because her purse holds only air and anxiety.
NORA 3	She unravels the top of the bag, licks a digit and dips it in. And she places that sugar-covered finger in her mouth where the taste of sweetness and sin allows her to escape. Just for a second.
NORA 2	She'd been taking the pills for a few months and when one didn't work, she took two and now, on the cusp of Christmas, she takes three. And as she places them on her tongue and swallows, the relief comes towards her like a liferaft.

NORA 1	She unscrews the top and takes a swig straight out the bottle. A little rush of rock and roll in amongst the managing and mothering. A little rush of rebellion.
THOMAS (*all*)	(*Offstage.*) Nora?
NORA (*all*)	Yes?
THOMAS 1	(*Offstage.*) Nora?
NORA 1	What?
	THOMAS *enters*.
THOMAS 1	You took your time.
NORA 1	Town was hectic.
THOMAS 1	I sent the kids to play next door.
NORA 1	I saw. They're out in her garden, you should have given them gloves.
THOMAS 1	They were driving me up the wall.
NORA 1	It's Christmas, what do you expect?
	THOMAS *looks at the tree*.
THOMAS 1	Is that the tree from last year?
NORA 1	It's nothing decorations won't fix.
THOMAS 1	Miracle-worker, are you?
NORA 1	It's got character.
THOMAS 1	That's just a nice way of saying it's fucking ugly.
NORA 1	It was half-price being so close to Christmas and everything.
THOMAS 1	Half-price? They should have paid you to take it away.
NORA 1	You'll need to get the decorations down from the cupboard. I can't reach them.

And don't look at me like that – I thought it would be nice to get a real tree.

THOMAS 1   Clearly.

NORA 1   Come on. Don't you think we should celebrate? I mean how many men on this street can say they've got a new job?

THOMAS 1   I don't start until January.

NORA 1   But how many can say they've got a brand-new job – starting in January. A brand-new – manager's job. How many men? None. And that's a fact. Though you'll need to start ironing your shirts. Which reminds me – let me show you where the iron is kept.

THOMAS 1   Isn't the ironing your job?

NORA 1   I tell you what, I'll iron your shirts, if you start hoovering or doing the dishes or making the kids' packed lunches or cleaning the bathroom or mopping the floors. Do you even know where we keep the bleach?

THOMAS 1   Yeah. It's... by the iron.

She shoots him a look.

Alright. I'll iron my own shirts.

NORA *moves close to* THOMAS.

NORA 1   But you know I am proud of you. You worked hard for that job. A few years ago, it would have been impossible for you, for us. But it seems like even in this shitty corner of the city, miracles are possible.

THOMAS 1   Oh, I know miracles are possible. Because I found you.

THOMAS *puts his hands around* NORA, *she pushes him off.*

NORA 1   You're such a sap. But I do think we should
              celebrate. Just… a little.

THOMAS 1   A little? I didn't know you even knew those
              words.

NORA 1   What's that meant to mean?

THOMAS 1   I know you. You're a little magpie.

NORA 1   You mean common?

THOMAS 1   No. You are anything but common. You
              are… a skylark.

NORA 1   And what's a skylark?

THOMAS 1   It's stunning. There are loads of them up
              north in the summer. It's meant to have one
              of the most beautiful… songs. A songbird.

              He puts his arms around her.

              You're my little songbird.

              They kiss. THOMAS *spots all her shopping
              bags.*

              And what is all this?

NORA 1   Nothing you need to know about.

THOMAS 1   Even though my money bought it? What is
              this /

NORA 1   No! That is a surprise.

THOMAS 1   For me?

NORA 1   Maybe.

THOMAS 1   Nora.

NORA 1   What?

THOMAS 1   You know what. All this – shit.

NORA 1   It's just a few things.

THOMAS 1	Just a few things?
NORA 1	I like /
THOMAS 1	Spending?
NORA 1	I just like /
THOMAS 1	Stuff. You like having stuff. I go through your pockets and you know what I find? Scratchcards. Like you're collecting them. Scratchcards and Lottery tickets. You're silly believing that /
NORA 1	You shouldn't go through my pockets.
THOMAS 1	And you shouldn't spend all our money, or didn't you notice all those red letters? You need to learn to keep yourself on the ground. Because half of this stuff is on your credit card, isn't it?

NORA *doesn't answer.*

And you know I hate that. I hate the borrowing and the scrabbling and the search for cash because if we're not careful… I just want us to be careful.

NORA 1	And I just want us to have a nice Christmas. For the first time in… I just want to us to have a nice Christmas.

For the kids.

Silence.

THOMAS 1	Okay. Alright.

THOMAS *goes into his pocket. Pulls out money and puts it in front of* NORA. *She goes to take it, he pulls it away from her before she get it. He laughs.*

That's not for spending on me or you. That's for the kids.

NORA 1	Gotcha. And thank you.
THOMAS 1	Shouldn't I get a kiss for that?
	NORA *hesitates, kisses him on the cheek.*
	And I suppose I should check what is it you want for Christmas or is that a secret too?
NORA 1	Oh. It's no secret. Just a little something... whatever you think you can... give.
THOMAS 1	Money isn't much of a gift.
NORA 1	Then I'll wrap it up in gold paper and hang it off the tree.
	She breathes on his neck. Almost kissing his lips. Teases him.
THOMAS 1	You've lies in the whites of your eyes, Nora. What have you done?
NORA 1	The only thing I've done is turn you on.
	NORA *goes to walk away,* THOMAS *grabs her.*
THOMAS 1	You know I can smell booze on your breath?
NORA 1	So, what?
THOMAS 1	So, sing for me. My little songbird.
	THOMAS *kisses her. They stop kissing.* *She tries to pull away, but he holds on to her.*
NORA 1	The kids could walk in.
THOMAS 1	I'll put the lock on.
NORA 1	But what if they /
THOMAS 1	Just relax.
	She tries to pull away, but he holds on to her.
NORA 1	I don't think it's /

THOMAS 1	I said just relax.
NORA 1	No, but /
THOMAS 1	Nora!
	NORA *pushes* THOMAS *away.*
NORA 1	We'll – later? Alright?
NORA 3	And she thinks of how her skin used to burn with his touch.
NORA 1	Of how he used to be all she wanted.
NORA 2	Of how much he wants her.
THOMAS 1	I am just trying to make you feel nice.
NORA 1	But don't you have some Christmas decorations to get?
THOMAS 1	But don't you want to fuck?
	Silence.
NORA 1	You're not meant to talk to me like that.
THOMAS 1	Fucking hell. These days it feels like there are more wrong things to say than right. You've been reading too many magazines with all those angry women in them. And stop worrying, will you? This year won't be like... I'm better now. Christmas will be fine.
NORA (*all*)	No. Christmas will be perfect.
	THOMAS *turns to leave.*
THOMAS 1	And by the way – you look beautiful in this light. Something how your hair just... you're lovely.
NORA (*all*)	Thank you.
	THOMAS *leaves.* NORA *watches him.*

NORA 1   And she stands in her living room
               surrounded by presents, she thinks of her
               husband's new employment.

NORA 3   As Director of the Bank.

NORA 2   As Head of Credit and Collections.

NORA 1   As Manager of a Short-Term Lender.

NORA 3   And for the first time in years she feels
               hope.

NORA 2   And as the feeling falls across her face,
               for a moment she becomes someone else,
               entirely.

NORA 3   Just for a blink.

NORA 1   She reveals the woman underneath.

               A knock at the door.

               Kids. I told you not to do that.

               She opens it.

               Oh. Sorry I thought you were…

CHRISTINE 1   Nora? Is that you? Nora Helmer? That is
               your married name isn't it? Am I saying
               it right?

NORA 1   Yeah?

CHRISTINE 1   You don't remember me? Do you?

NORA 1   I'm sorry I…

CHRISTINE 1   In all fairness, it's been – what – nearly ten
               years?

NORA 1   No, I… No. Can't be.

CHRISTINE 1   Am I that different?

NORA 1   Christine!?

CHRISTINE 1   Nora!

NORA 1	Oh my god… Christine. You've… you've changed… you've… what am I doing – you're here! Come in. Come in from the cold. Take off your jacket. Warm up it's so… cold.
	CHRISTINE enters the living room.
	Now I see. I see – you. But you've lost weight? You're half the girl /
CHRISTINE 1	I'm not a girl, Nora. I'm older, we both are.
NORA 1	Just a little older. Maybe. Just a tiny bit.
CHRISTINE 1	I know you shouldn't turn up without asking but I thought it would be fun for my visit to be a surprise – so, surprise!
	She takes off her jacket. NORA *stares at her. Silence.*
	You're quiet.
NORA 1	I'm sorry. It's just a shock. I suddenly feel a hundred years old.
CHRISTINE 1	Well, you don't look it. Barely look a day older. Are those kids out there yours?
NORA 1	Yeah.
CHRISTINE 1	Fucking hell. Three?
NORA 1	Yeah.
CHRISTINE 1	Fucking hell.
NORA 1	Yeah. You've kids?
CHRISTINE 1	God, no. I killed a cactus last week – which I didn't know was even possible. I'm fancy-free and loving it.
NORA 1	Loving it?
CHRISTINE 1	Why wouldn't I be?

NORA 1	Yeah, course. A drink? A coffee? A tea? A whisky? Anything – I can't stand someone with empty hands.
CHRISTINE 1	No, I'm fine.
NORA 1	Are you hungry? I haven't got much in, but I can make some /
CHRISTINE 1	No, I'm fine.
NORA 1	A glass of water?
CHRISTINE 1	I'm fine.
NORA 1	Are you sure? I might even have some /
CHRISTINE 1	It's okay. Don't fuss. No need to do a single thing. Just sit with me... I want to see you. Just you.

Silence.

NORA 1	Let me get you that glass of water.

NORA *exits.* CHRISTINE *enters.*

CHRISTINE 2	I like your kitchen, Nora. It's very... yellow. I mean that wallpaper is certainly... something.
NORA 2	It's a little old-fashioned but Tom likes it that way. Are you sure I can't get you a drink, Christine? A festive tipple?
CHRISTINE 2	It's a little too early for a whisky lemonade – do you still drink them?
NORA 2	I've been known to.
CHRISTINE 2	Good. I really hope you haven't changed a bit, Nora. You were always so – lovely.
NORA 2	When was it I last saw you?
CHRISTINE 2	It was the year my mother died. I remember it. You came to her funeral wearing this bright-red lipstick.

NORA 2	Well, that sounds totally inappropriate.
CHRISTINE 2	No, it was beautiful. You looked… so, that would have been 1960. In a blink half a century will have passed. I'm sure of it. So, you must tell me – everything. Tell me happy stories, your stories were always filled with such happiness.
NORA 2	Well. Tom is about to start a new job – in a bank. He looks after those new credit cards, have you seen them? Little miracles, really.
CHRISTINE 2	Yeah. I've heard about them. Very modern.
NORA 2	And I'm very proud of him. He worked, well, he worked very hard for it – had to do all these courses and whatnot. I can't help but feel our future is a little more, secure. Do you know what I mean?
CHRISTINE 2	I know exactly what you mean. But I find it hard to imagine a time when your future wasn't secure. You have always been blessed with luck.
NORA 2	It's true I've been lucky in many ways.
CHRISTINE 2	In every way.
NORA 2	Not quite.
CHRISTINE 2	What do you mean?
NORA 2	It doesn't matter.
CHRISTINE 2	Nora?
NORA 2	I thought you wanted happy stories.
CHRISTINE 2	And after all these years, I would like to hear the truth too.
NORA 2	I'd choose happiness over the truth, wouldn't you?
CHRISTINE 2	No.

NORA 2   No? No. Yes. Of course. I was just being –
                    silly.

                    Do you have a man? Or are you in the
                    market for a boyfriend?

CHRISTINE 2   Not particularly.

NORA 2   Oh. Then you must work?

CHRISTINE 2   Yes, bookkeeping and such. Though it's
                    getting tougher to find, I fear I am not
                    exactly what employers are looking for.
                    And I'd get one of those new credit cards
                    except they still make it so hard for a
                    woman to… never mind.

NORA 2   I've got an idea. Tom is bound to be looking
                    for staff at some point – I could ask him if
                    there might be something for you?

CHRISTINE 2   No. I wouldn't ask that of you.

NORA 2   Please. Let me help you? Let me help an old
                    friend. It's no trouble.

CHRISTINE 2   Well, then… thank you. Thank you. If there
                    was a little something for me, I would
                    gladly take it.

NORA 2   Then I'll ask him. You must feel very proud
                    to work. I've never… I've never.

CHRISTINE 2   I like it. It gives me – options. And it also
                    gives me purpose. Because the truth is
                    sometimes, Nora. Sometimes I feel so…
                    I feel ever so, well, you know.

NORA 2   No. I don't.

CHRISTINE 2   Tell me then, what are you most proud of?
                    Your children?

NORA 2   Yes. I suppose.

CHRISTINE 2   You're uncertain?

NORA 2	No. Well…
CHRISTINE 2	Do I sense a secret?
NORA 2	No, I…
CHRISTINE 2	Tell me! We must always talk the truth to each other.
NORA 2	Well. If we are talking of the truth.
CHRISTINE 2	Always.
NORA 2	You're right. The thing I feel most proud of is – a secret. A secret, that if I am going to share it, you must swear to keep it and not even share it with your shadow.
CHRISTINE 2	I swear.
NORA 2	And she explains that there was a time when her husband was very ill. He lay in bed for months, unable and fading – for reasons that fail her.
NORA 3	Because it was something to do with the pressure of the world changing. He had spent just a few months in France, far enough away from the front line so as to keep all his fingers. But it seems part of him had been damaged because he never did stop jumping at the sound of doors slamming.
NORA 2	The Swinging Sixties seem to have swung in a direction away from him. The traditions he clung on to were crumbling, so he found himself stumbling to find his place in this new landscape.
NORA 1	Because magazines and the TV and the internet and just about everyone he met reminded him of all the things he lacked. Because he didn't own his house or his car and even their furniture was on credit.

	Which meant there was nothing for him to hold on to when he fell into a state of sadness.
NORA 3	Simply put – he fell apart and so did their finances. And even their savings shrivelled up soon enough.
NORA 1	But they kept on spending and selling the lie that everything was fine.
NORA 2	Because she didn't want her children to worry.
NORA 3	And she didn't want her neighbours to know.
NORA 1	And as she tells her friend of her husband's difficulties and their debt, water wets her eyes, but she is determined not to cry.
CHRISTINE 2	That's awful, Nora. How did you keep it all together? How did you… keep all this?
NORA 2	I used to tell people – it was my inheritance seeing us through those dark times. My father had just died, you see, and I said his wallet was our protection. When actually he died without much to his name.
CHRISTINE 2	Oh, I'm so /
NORA 2	It was me. I raised that money. I – and I alone – covered our bills and expenses and… everything. For months and months, I didn't just keep a home, I ran it. I ran this whole household – like a man. And that, is what I am most proud of and I've never told anyone, until now.
CHRISTINE 2	I'm honoured that you told me. And that's incredible. I mean – that must have been a huge amount of money. How did you get it?
NORA 2	Well, I arranged to – wait. No. That. That I won't say. Some secrets – must stay secrets. I must be careful not to get too giddy.

CHRISTINE 2	Why? You haven't done something silly? Have you? To get the money.
NORA 2	Is it silly to save your whole family?
CHRISTINE 2	Then why lie and say it's your father's money? And am I right in saying, not even Tom knows about this? Nora. What have you done?
NORA 2	I did what I had to.
CHRISTINE 2	And what is that?
	NORA *remains silent. She smiles and shrugs.*
NORA 2	It is amazing what you can be capable of, when you try.
CHRISTINE 2	And I never knew you were capable of such secrets.
NORA 2	I felt capable. Christine. In secrecy and silence, I saved my whole family and maybe for the first time in my life, I felt capable.
CHRISTINE 2	Well, that's a wonderful thing. And it's brave. What you have done, for your husband, your children.
NORA 2	Do you really think that?
CHRISTINE 2	I think being brave can look like many things and most of them are unexpected.
NORA 2	Oh, I have missed you. I have missed having someone to talk to.
	Silence.
CHRISTINE 2	I suddenly need a cigarette. Do you mind?
NORA 2	No, of course not.
CHRISTINE 2	I shall go out to the garden – would hate to ruin this lovely smell. Lavender? Is it?

NORA 2   Yes. Lavender. You saw the door through
                the kitchen?

                CHRISTINE *nods and turns to leave.*

                And Christine? Why today? Why visit
                today, after all this time.

CHRISTINE 2   I am visiting an old friend of my mother's
                and I'd heard you lived nearby and I…
                I was always so sad we had fallen out of
                touch. I missed you. I suppose, I missed
                you. I won't be a moment.

                CHRISTINE *leaves. A knock at the door.*
                NORA *answers the door – it's* NATHAN.

NORA 3   Mr McKinnon.

NATHAN 3   Good afternoon, Mrs Helmer.

NORA 3   What brings you to my door?

NATHAN 3   I am here to talk to your husband. I believe
                he is to be above me in the bank. So, I want
                to wish him well.

NORA 3   And that is the only reason for your visit?

NATHAN 3   You will raise suspicion if you look any more
                concerned about my arrival, Mrs Helmer.

NORA 3   And what would I have to be suspicious
                about?

NATHAN 3   Then are you not better to place a smile on
                your face?

NORA 3   I always have a smile on my face, Mr
                McKinnon.

NATHAN 3   Then won't you invite me in? There is
                a sharp chill in the air.

                NORA *reluctantly lets him in.*

                That river is set to freeze over. You should
                be mindful of your children playing near it.

NORA 3	How thoughtful of you to mention that to me.
NATHAN 3	I'm surprised that weather did not stop you ladies from voting.
NORA 3	It would have taken more than a little chill to stop us from voting for the first time.
NATHAN 3	It seems as though this year has turned out to be a year for the history books. They will be writing about it until the next century.
NORA 3	Women voting and the end of a war are things certainly worth celebrating. Remind me, where was it you served, Mr McKinnon?
NATHAN 3	Have we not had this conversation before?
NORA 3	It must have slipped my mind.
NATHAN 3	Unfortunately, I did not get the opportunity to serve my country, on account of my /
NORA 3	Failings?
NATHAN 3	Children. Widowers with children were exempt from service. Tell me, did you enjoy your first fluttering with the vote?
NORA 3	Yes. I did.
NATHAN 3	You'll do well to remember that politics are a mirage. They make you think that you can change things. When you cannot.
NORA 3	Clearly that isn't true.
NATHAN 3	But how many times have I voted and how many times have I got the country I wanted?
NORA 3	Mr Helmer is in the back room.
NATHAN 3	Is my talk not small enough for someone like /
NORA 3	Thomas is in the back room.
NATHAN 3	Thank you, Nora.

NATHAN *leaves.* NORA *is left for a moment.*

CHRISTINE *enters.*

CHRISTINE 3   Oh, Nora. Your kitchen is lovely. Very... yellow. That wallpaper is certainly... something.

NORA 3   Thank you, Christine. It's a little old-fashioned but Thomas likes it that way

CHRISTINE 3   There is a sudden chill in here.

NORA 3   I had the door open.

CHRISTINE 3   A visitor?

NORA 3   A Mr McKinnon.

CHRISTINE 3   Nathan?

NORA 3   You know him?

CHRISTINE 3   I used to... many years ago. It appears my past is surrounding me.

DANIEL *walks in from the room next door.*

DANIEL 3   (*Calling back to* THOMAS.) I shall see myself out.

NORA 3   Daniel! You've appeared like magic.

DANIEL 3   A simple trick, I slipped in the back door. When I looked through the window and I saw you both talking I did not wish to get in the way.

NORA 3   Oh, but you are always welcome here. Christine, this is our friend Daniel. He lives just around this corner. He works at the chemist and helps keep us all fighting fit. And this is Christine, an old friend.

CHRISTINE 3   It is lovely to meet you.

DANIEL 3   And a pleasure to finally meet you. I've heard so much about you.

NORA 3	Can you believe it's been a nearly a century since I last saw her.
CHRISTINE 3	You mean nearly a decade, Nora.
NORA 3	Of course, how foolish of me.
DANIEL 3	Speaking of fools, your husband is entertaining the company of one.
CHRISTINE 3	Nathan McKinnon?
DANIEL 3	Walked straight in on us in the middle of our conversation. Not even a knock. He wished to congratulate Thomas on his new position in the bank. You'll do well not to let him visit again. Mr McKinnon rather has a reputation.
CHRISTINE 3	Do we not all have reputations?
DANIEL 3	His wife drank herself to death, drowned in cheap gin. He was left alone with his two children. Barely managing to /
NORA 3	Enough. We should be celebrating the end of this tremendous year. In fact, we've absolutely no choice – let us raise a glass of something.
DANIEL 3	I thought you were trying to drink a little less?
NORA 3	Christine brought it.
CHRISTINE 3	Did I?
NORA 3	Let us all have one – two at most. But three does sound like fun.
	NORA *reaches into her shopping and pulls out the bottle of alcohol, pours them all a drink.*
	Let us raise a toast to peacetime.
CHRISTINE 3	And progress.

DANIEL 3	And pals.
NORA 3	Pals? What a word, Daniel. But what a wonderful word.
ALL	To peacetime, progress and pals!
	They savour it. THOMAS *enters holding his jacket.*
NORA 3	Shhhhhh…
	NORA *quietly and playfully hides the bottle.*
THOMAS 3	Do I sense secrets?
NORA 3	No such thing.
DANIEL 3	Did you get rid of him?
THOMAS 3	I walked him out the back door. Are you having a tipple?
	NORA *quickly interjects.*
NORA 3	Thomas, please let me introduce you to Christine – a friend from school.
THOMAS 3	I do not believe we've met.
	THOMAS *and* CHRISTINE *shake hands.*
CHRISTINE 3	I have heard a lot about you.
THOMAS 3	I should hope nothing but kind words.
NORA 3	Of course! In fact, she has travelled all this way just to meet you.
CHRISTINE 3	Well…
NORA 3	Christine has always been good with numbers – ever since we were children. And she is looking for a job that she could grow into and better herself. I thought maybe you are the very person to help her. I have never

	known someone get so far on their own steam as you – brilliant you. Do you think there might be something for her?
THOMAS 3	You have experience of bookkeeping?
CHRISTINE 3	Plenty.
THOMAS 3	And you have no husband or /
CHRISTINE 3	No. I am alone, in those respects.
THOMAS 3	Well. You will need to interview of course but I am certain we can organise something.
NORA 3	I knew it.
CHRISTINE 3	Oh, how can I thank you?
THOMAS 3	There is no need to. But I do need to go the bank I have more files to collect and read. By the time I start in January I need to know the place like I was born in the boardroom.
NORA 3	You work so ceaselessly for us.
THOMAS 3	Like any husband or father, would or should.
DANIEL 3	I'll walk with you.
THOMAS 3	Are you on your way to work, Daniel?
DANIEL 3	No. I... I am due a day off.
THOMAS 3	Quite right. You work so hard and are looking tired for it.
DANIEL 3	It's true, I have been tired recently. But nothing your company does not fix.
	THOMAS *and* CHRISTINE *puts on their jackets.*
CHRISTINE 3	I should also be on my way.
NORA 3	I could make up a bed for you here?

CHRISTINE 3   You have done more than enough for me.
               I'm staying with a friend of my mother's.
               It's very nearby.

DANIEL 3   Until tomorrow.

NORA 3   Until tomorrow. And Christine, shall I see
               you tomorrow? Will you come by?

CHRISTINE 3   That would be lovely.

THOMAS 3   Nora, will you fetch the children? You know
               how I hate them playing down by that river.
               It is an accident waiting to happen.

NORA 3   Yes. Of course. Goodbye. Stay warm.

THOMAS 3   So long, skylark.

               THOMAS *kisses her on the forehead.*
               THOMAS, CHRISTINE *and* DANIEL
               leave, talking.

NORA 3   A woman's finger falls to her wrist and she
               feels a small cut from only a few days ago.
               A small cut from when she stood in the
               ballot box and for the first time had her
               future at her fingertips. She gripped that
               pencil so tight her thumb went numb. The
               lead snapped as she placed it on the paper.
               And she marked it with her heart and her
               head and her hope. She marked it with hope.
               Then she rolled down her glove and took
               the piece of paper and gently glided it along
               her skin. A thin sting of red, rose to the
               surface. A paper cut. She ensured it was
               deep enough to scar as she thought of that
               woman lying dead in front of a horse and
               a king, so she could stand here and for the
               very first time have her future at her
               fingertips. She stared at the red ribbon of
               blood that lined the bottom of her ballot
               paper and wondered about all the things we

was willing to bleed for – 'Oh, silly me' is what she said when she got home, and pretended it was an accident. 'Oh, silly me.'

A knock at the door. NORA *opens it – it's* NATHAN.

NORA 1   Nathan? Twice in one day. Lucky me.

NATHAN 1   I'm just /

NORA 1   He isn't home. Tommy's gone into town.

NATHAN 1   It isn't him I'm after. It's you.

              NORA *hesitates. She lets him in.*

              That woman? That woman who just left here... that was Christine. Wasn't it?

NORA 1   So, what if it was?

NATHAN 1   Heard she is going through hard times. Heard she is struggling to find work, lost her man too.

NORA 1   People go through hard times, Nathan. It's what they do – they go through hard times.

NATHAN 1   You know what I also heard?

NORA 1   That you're a good listener?

NATHAN 1   You're quick.

NORA 1   And you're not quick enough because I need to get my kids indoors.

NATHAN 1   Your husband doesn't think much of me. That's what I heard. He proved as much this afternoon. Hardly said two things and he was shoving me out the door. Rumour has it when he starts, he is going to fire some folk – something about letting go of old history.

NORA 1   What's this got to do with me?

NATHAN 1   Well. When I see Christine is busy walking
              down the street with your husband, I can't
              help but feel she is looking for a new man
              or a new job. And you're still wearing your
              wedding ring.

NORA 1   Don't you think you're jumping to
              conclusions?

NATHAN 1   No. I know how the world works. You only
              get pulled up and out of the shit if you know
              the hand doing the pulling. And I just want
              to make sure my job is safe and I'm not
              losing it, so Christine can get hers.

NORA 1   I'm not… how can you expect me to /

NATHAN 1   Just say you'll help.

NORA 1   Help how?

NATHAN 1   Just say you'll help me.

NORA (*all*) There is nothing I can do.

NATHAN 1   Are you sure about that?

NORA 1   Why?

NATHAN 1   Here. Take this.

              NATHAN *holds out a document*. NORA
              takes it.

NORA 3   And he hands her a document. Ready for
              this moment when…

NORA 2   This moment when /

NORA 1   This moment when /

NATHAN 1   I know what you did. And here is the proof.

              NORA *opens the envelope and looks at the
              pieces of paper. She stands – shocked.*

NORA 3   And in her hand was a copy of a loan
              agreement.

NORA 2	A successful credit-card application.
NORA 1	A payday-loan contract.
NORA (*all*)	What is this?
NATHAN 1	Those papers were signed by your dad. We got his application in the post. He clearly needed a lot of cash and quickly. Which is surprising because I checked the dates and dying men don't tend to need so much money.
NORA 1	They must have got the dates wrong.
NORA 2	And he never was very good with his finances.
NORA 3	So, why are you showing this to me?
NATHAN 1	The papers were submitted just days before he died and wasn't he terribly sick? And if he was anything like my father, I bet he wasn't even conscious in those final days. It wouldn't take much to find out and it wouldn't take much to counterfeit a dying man's signature.
NORA (*all*)	What?
NATHAN 1	Not to mention there is a trail of unsuccessful applications in your name. You couldn't get the money – so you pretended to be him. It's easy enough to prove you committed fraud, Nora. I know you're a thief.
NORA 3	Forged.
NORA 2	Faked.
NORA 1	Fucked.
	NORA *rips up the letter.*
NATHAN 1	You think that's the only copy?

NORA 1   You're blackmailing me?

NATHAN 1   It's clever really, what you did.

NORA 1   How did you know?

NATHAN 1   I've got access to all the accounts. Trust me, information is easy to find when you go looking. And, don't look at me like that, not like that, because I'm not the one looking at time in prison.

NORA (*all*)   Prison?

NATHAN 1   Minimum two years, but it could be more. Or maybe, they'd just put you under house arrest, but I wonder if they'd take away your kids? Regardless, I imagine a criminal record could really fuck things up for you. Not to mention your husband's new job.

NORA (*all*)   Oh my god.

NATHAN 1   And I'll show everyone what you did. I'll show everyone who you really are. Unless I can keep my job.

NORA 1   But it's just a job and this is my whole life.

NATHAN 1   You're right it's a stupid shit job that makes poor people poorer. But do you know how long it took me to get that fucking job? A lifetime. A whole fucking lifetime. Don't let them take that away from me.

NORA 1   But I don't know how to help you.

NATHAN 1   Then find a way.

NORA 1   But... please... I never wanted to... I was just trying to... Tommy was sick and we had bills to pay and quickly and... I was trying to... I was desperate.

NATHAN 1	Oh. I know. I know what desperate is. Everyone around here knows what desperate is and I don't want to hurt you, Nora. All I want to be is a good father, with a good job but the world makes that so fucking hard.
NORA 1	The world makes lots of things fucking hard. So, please. Please don't do this… I'll do anything. Please. I'll do anything you want. Anything… please. If you want someone… I'd sleep with you – you can do anything you want to me – fuck me however you want, I don't care… I don't care… please, just /
NATHAN 1	Once you know my job is safe, Nora. You can come and tell me. You come and knock on my door and tell me the good news. And I'll destroy any proof of… anything. That way we're both safe. And you'll know what door to knock, it's the only yellow door on the street. You know, I fucking hate it but it was my wife's favourite colour. She painted that door and my kids won't let me /
NORA 1	But what about my kids?
NATHAN 1	And what about mine. Because I will do anything to keep them safe. They are the only reason, the only reason, I haven't drowned myself in that river. I imagine you'd say the same.

Silence.

NORA 1	If I got money – could I pay you off? If not the job… then money?
NATHAN 1	It would need to be a hell of a lot of money. Double, triple, what you borrowed.

NORA 1	That's impossible.
NATHAN 1	Then make sure I keep my job.
NORA 1	Please.
NATHAN 1	Stop begging. Your husband might treat you like one, but you're not a dog.
NORA 1	But... please.
NATHAN 1	Money is fucking awful isn't it? The things it does to us. The things it's already done.

NATHAN hesitates.

I'm going to leave now, but I'm wanting to hear from you soon. Merry Christmas. Nora.

NATHAN leaves. NORA is left.

NORA 2	A criminal.
NORA 3	Everything?
NORA 1	I just...
NORA 2	The children...
NORA 1	I just...
NORA 3	We'd lose everything.
NORA 2	I can't.
NORA 1	I just...
NORA (*all*)	What have I done?

Silence. THOMAS enters.

THOMAS 3	The children are asking for you. You really should not let them play outdoors for so long. Did you have company?

NORA shakes her head.

Are you sure... because I walked past Mr McKinnon. Fresh snow, Nora. His footprints led back to here.

NORA 3   He stepped in for a few minutes.

THOMAS 3   Did he mention he is worried about the
                security of his employment? And asked you
                to put in a good word for him? Your face,
                my songbird. It tells me truths.

NORA 3   Does it?

                She turns away from him.

THOMAS 3   I say that in jest, Nora. I heard at the bank
                he has been voicing concerns about his
                position. But you were not going to tell me
                he visited, were you? You should be careful,
                secrets and lies are like damp. Once they are
                in the woodwork, the whole house is
                condemned. And don't allow yourself to
                believe that there is a scrap of human in
                him. He would happily tread on anyone if
                he thought it helped him.

NORA 3   Do you think he would harm someone?
                Really, truly?

THOMAS 3   Oh, my little songbird, life in this sitting
                room is very different to life on a street.
                In here is a haven and I am thankful for it.
                Thankful for you.

NORA 3   Thomas?

THOMAS 3   What?

NORA 3   What did he do? Why does everyone seem
                to dislike him so?

THOMAS 3   He bankrupted his whole family. Not to
                mention his wife drank her life away. Poor
                life choices.

NORA 3   He sounds desperate.

THOMAS 3   Morally bankrupt if you ask me.

NORA 3	But it seems he can keep a job and raise his two children.
THOMAS 3	Those children have been affected by their father's terrible choices. I mean poor parenting leaves very particular scars – do you not you think? Look what our fathers did to us.
NORA 3	I loved my father.
THOMAS 3	But do we not love people despite their flaws?
NORA 3	Or because of them?
THOMAS 3	You always reach for the positive no matter how implausible. Which is why I am so pleased our children have you. They are only around your goodness and sweetness. Not contaminated by someone else's terrible choices. And regardless, I'm going to ask for Mr Nathan McKinnon to be dismissed in the new year.
NORA (*all*)	No.
THOMAS 3	Yes.
NORA 3	No. You can't. You can't do that.
THOMAS 3	Why should it concern you?
NORA 2	Please, Thomas.
NORA 1	You've got to give him a second chance.
THOMAS 3	He isn't worth your worry.
NORA (*all*)	No.
THOMAS 3	Nora.
NORA 3	No.
THOMAS 3	Nora.

NORA 1	Please don't.
NORA 2	Please.
NORA 3	You can't.
THOMAS 3	Nora – keep calm. You'll make yourself panicked and recently, you have been very good at keeping yourself calm. And it speaks to your kindness that you could care so much about the fate of stranger. But you must forget him.

And don't frown, it will give you wrinkles.

Silence.

NORA 3	Thomas?
THOMAS 3	Yes?
NORA 3	There has been... I seemed to have... I have...
THOMAS 3	You must be tired from your day. You can barely string two words together.
NORA 3	I need your help.
THOMAS 3	I already said I would bring down the decorations when I had time.
NORA 3	No. It's...
THOMAS 3	What? I have enough to stew on without your silly little worries.

Silence. NORA *hesitates.*

NORA 3	A dress. For the party we are attending. It's only two days away and I do not know what to wear.
THOMAS 3	No need to go watery-eyed at the thought of picking a dress. I will help you. But first – a drink. And call in the children, won't you.

	They should come in, be around you and your warmth.
	THOMAS *leaves. Silence.*
NORA 1	A woman stands alone in her sitting room. Surprised by how destructive she has been.
NORA 2	How in attempting to save everything she has snapped it.
NORA 3	In silence and secrecy she has destroyed, everything.
NORA 1	And she is astounded by her own power.
NORA 2	She never knew she had it in her.
NORA 3	My skeleton.
NORA 2	My ribcage.
NORA 1	My heart.
NORA 3	As if /
NORA 1	As if /
NORA 3	As if it was enough just to feel it.
NORA 2	As if it was enough just to feel it to stop it.
NORA 1	Can feel myself pollute.
NORA 3	Can feel myself turn to poison at the thought.
NORA 1	From milk into madness and back again.
NORA 2	Curdling and turning and craving. As if my hands were enough to hold back any hurt.
NORA 3	As if my hands were /
NORA 2	Would dig through all of hellfire.
NORA 1	Would walk barefooted through sleet and snow.

NORA 2	Would do /
NORA 3	Would do just about /
NORA 1	My heart beats for /
NORA (*all*)	My heart beats for you.
NORA 1	And as she thinks of her children.
NORA 3	She thinks of the river.
NORA 2	She thinks of being washed clean.
NORA 1	Stay out there, kids. Play as long as you'd like.
NORA 2	Children. It's good to get fresh air.
NORA 3	My sweethearts. Keep playing.
NORA (*all*)	Be careful of that river and just stay out there. Stay away from me.

DAY TWO

NORA 2

A woman walks into her living room after
a sleepless dreamless night to find that her
children had got up early to make a
Christmas card just for her. It's all glue and
glitter and their attempts at artistry pull at
parts of her that feel like the most fragile.
It's been years since she stood outside the
doctor's office with her hand on her stomach.
For the third time something was growing
inside of her. The third time – no monthly
bleeding, the morning sickness, a tiredness
trapped in every tendon. There was a sense of
purpose she enjoyed about being pregnant.
But sometimes she just felt like a body that
needed prodded and measured and ripped
open when the time was right. And she knew
that more mouths need more money. More
money meant less of her husband and less of
her husband meant… well, an afternoon can
feel like a precariously long time when you
are the only adult. And when that third child
arrived, through a slit in her stomach. It took
twenty-six stitches to sew her up. Stitches
that she picked at, and although it hurt, she
still played with the strands that stuck out of
her. All dried blood and sore skin. Now, a
scar stretched and stubborn sits there on her
stomach. Her husband won't touch it, but it
still fascinates her. And she thinks about how
a human can heal from being torn in two.
And as tears fill her eyes and her children
question why, she replies – 'Mummy is just
being silly, just being silly.'

CHRISTINE 2	Afternoon, Nora!
NORA 2	Oh, Christine.
CHRISTINE 2	It's just me. No need to be alarmed.
NORA 2	I've been a million miles away all day.
CHRISTINE 2	Is everything fine?
NORA 2	I am... overwhelmingly fine. Did you see the children playing? They insisted on going outside again to finish whatever game they were playing yesterday. I watch them from the window, how I wish I could play pretend like they do. I actually wanted to ask you something. We are going to a party tomorrow and I want to wear a very particular dress, but the trouble is last time I wore it I managed to catch it on /
CHRISTINE 2	It won't take me long with a needle and thread to sort that out.
NORA 2	You were always so much more practical than me.
CHRISTINE 2	While walking here I saw your friend – Daniel? He looked... well... I can't say he looked very well at all.
NORA 2	Lately he has had a cough and an ache he cannot shake.
CHRISTINE 2	I did wonder if he was your mysterious benefactor. I noticed he wasn't wearing a wedding ring. Unless of course... he prefers the company of other men.
NORA 2	Christine. You've jumped to a very particular conclusion.
CHRISTINE 2	It's been legal a whole year, Nora. And around a lot longer than that. Is it really so bad for two men to share a life? If anything

	wouldn't it do us a favour if men lived with each other rather than us.
NORA 2	Well... I find it hard to imagine, is all.
CHRISTINE 2	You are behind the times we live in, Nora. We don't have to live the life of our mothers. Just look around, abortions – above board – for the first time, this very year. And the contraceptive pill too, to stop children happening in the first place. Which is as close to a miracle as I will see this lifetime.
NORA 2	It is amazing to think you can undo a child. Such options, such options I never had.
CHRISTINE 2	What do you mean... do you think you might have /
NORA 2	No. Of course not. It's just... I was so terribly sad after the children were born. Sadness three times. I only just feel like I am returning to myself – after all these years and now... and now...
CHRISTINE 2	Has something happened since yesterday? You seem a little... undone.
	Long silence.
NORA 2	I've laid everything out in the kitchen, everything you'll need to fix the dress.
CHRISTINE 2	Are you... are you alright /
NORA 2	Please make some tea or some coffee or a glass of whatever. I do appreciate your help.
CHRISTINE 2	Nora...
	Silence. THOMAS *enters, carrying folders and files. He places them down.*
NORA 2	My darling! You took your time!
THOMAS 2	It is rather icy out there.

CHRISTINE 2	More files to study, Tom?
THOMAS 2	It seems to be never-ending and I managed to forget my briefcase at home. My head is so full of facts and figures.
CHRISTINE 2	Then I'll leave you be and get to that sewing.
NORA 2	Thank you, Christine.
	CHRISTINE *exits*.
	I've invited her over to help fix my dress.
THOMAS 2	So, I chose well?
NORA 2	Yes. I'm glad I gave in to you.
THOMAS 2	Gave in to me?
NORA 2	I didn't mean /
THOMAS 2	I know what you meant.
NORA 2	You're working?
THOMAS 2	Of course. I still have so much to catch up on and January is less than two weeks away. And then our life will change, won't it?
NORA 2	I hope it doesn't change too much.
THOMAS 2	Well, of course. A new year, a new job, a beautiful wife and three fine children. What more could a man want.
NORA 2	It's... amazing. Isn't it? You've got everything you've ever wanted.
NORA (*all*)	And I am so proud of you.
THOMAS 2	What do you want?
NORA (*all*)	You are so suspicious.
THOMAS 2	Something tells me I have the right to be suspicious. What is it my songbird wants?
NORA 2	Would you be willing to grant me a wish? One last wish before the year is out.

THOMAS 2	What is it?
NORA 2	I'd be willing to do just about anything for it.
NORA 3	Your little skylark would sing for you – any song you wanted.
NORA 1	It's just a favour. I am not asking for a miracle.
THOMAS 2	Then what? What is it that has you fluttering?
NORA 2	Please... please will you let Mr McKinnon keep his job?
THOMAS 2	I am giving his job to Christine – isn't that what you wanted?
NORA 2	But isn't there room for both of them? Can't you get rid of someone else.
THOMAS 2	You know I do not understand you, Nora. Have you promised him something which I cannot deliver?
NORA 2	Who knows what he will say about you, he could spread lies and untruths. If he is as bad as you believe he is – why would you anger him? I don't think he would stop short of slandering your whole name.
NORA 3	We don't know what people are capable of – they could dig up anything, make up anything. Please, Thomas. Think of me, think of the children...
THOMAS 3	I am not scared of him.
NORA (*all*)	Then please listen.
THOMAS 3	This is getting tiring.
NORA 3	You cannot dismiss a man who is good at his job. That is immoral.

THOMAS 3   Then what if I am making structural
                changes? Structural changes to his
                department. He cannot have his job if it no
                longer exists. And of course, he is free to
                apply for another position, but I imagine
                Christine, might have a little better luck, in
                fact why don't I just...

NORA 3   Thomas? What are you doing?

THOMAS 3   I shall get them to inform him of his notice
                period. I do not imagine there will be much
                resistance and it's one less task for January
                and you might finally stop mentioning him.

NORA 3   But it's Christmas and you haven't officially
                started your /

THOMAS 3   And this is business and trust me, people
                will be glad he is gone.

NORA 3   Please. Do not do this. Do not do this. You
                do not realise what this could do please.

                NORA *grabs on to* THOMAS.

                You have no idea what this could do.

                THOMAS *shrugs off* NORA.

THOMAS 3   Oh please.

NORA 3   Do not, Thomas.

                NORA *grabs on to* THOMAS *again.*

THOMAS 3   Stop it.

NORA 3   You don't know what this will do.

THOMAS 3   I said stop it.

NORA 3   You don't know /

THOMAS 3   And I said /

NORA (*all*)   Stop.

	NORA *slaps* THOMAS. *Both are in shock. He backs away. She moves towards him.*
THOMAS 3	Nora.
NORA 3	Thomas, I am so sorry. I am so sorry. Forgive me. I was overwhelmed… something overwhelmed me, I… didn't mean to hurt you. I'm…
THOMAS 3	I do not… imagine the children walked in?
NORA 3	I am so sorry. I am so sorry for what I have done.
	NORA *drops to her knees. Silence.*
THOMAS 3	What has gotten into you? What is with all this hysteria? You are acting like a madwoman over something which does not concern you.
NORA 3	I just… what if I were to tell you something. Something which… would change everything. Something which would… disappoint you. Greatly disappoint you.
THOMAS 3	Oh, please. Nora. I already know.
NORA (*all*)	What do you mean?
THOMAS 3	I already know, my little skylark. You cannot keep secrets from me.
	THOMAS *picks up* NORA.
	There is no need to get dirt on your knees.
NORA 3	You know?
THOMAS 3	Of course, I know.
	I know the children broke my mother's porcelain doll. I saw the chips on the floor last week and then I saw it was missing…
NORA 3	Oh.

THOMAS 3	Accidents happen. Even I can appreciate that. Is this what this is all this about? Is it? The air of guilt. The mania. All this madness over a broken doll. I know that you are very sensitive to these things. But this... this is out of all proportion. For you are not capable of true terribleness, Nora. I know that. Even the thought that you might be capable of a second of badness... it makes my whole heart hurt, like I am on the brink of a heart attack.
NORA 3	Do not say that.
THOMAS 3	You are goodness through and through, a delicate goodness. Like that little porcelain doll.
NORA 1	Tommy... I'm...
NORA (*all*)	I'm sorry.
NORA 2	I never meant to cause any... trouble.
THOMAS 2	How could I stay angry at that face? Now, what was I going to do... yes, Mr Nathan McKinnon. I do hope he goes without too much fuss. I'll come back and put away those files and folders once I'm finished my phone call and, in the meantime, you should settle yourself. Maybe you should take one of your pills. Stop you from flying away.
	THOMAS *exits*. NORA *is left*.
NORA 1	Must settle myself.
NORA 3	Must still my soul.
NORA 2	Silence these thoughts.
NORA 1	Silence these feelings.
NORA 3	Drown it out.
NORA 2	Flood it out.

NORA 1	Stop thinking these thoughts.
NORA (*all*)	Must drown it out.
	A knock on the door. NORA *takes several large breaths and opens it. It's* DANIEL.
NORA 1	Danny.
DANIEL 1	Mind if I step in?
NORA 1	I'm actually… I'm in the middle of something.
DANIEL 1	Oh, right. It's just I… I saw the kids outside and figured you'd like some company.
NORA 1	I thought they might burn off some excess energy playing out here.
DANIEL 1	Oh, yeah. Sure…
NORA 1	Shouldn't you be at work?
DANIEL 1	Got someone to cover my shift at the chemist because it's just I…
NORA 1	You alright, Danny?
DANIEL 1	No. Not really.
	Silence. NORA *hesitates.*
NORA 1	Come in. I wasn't… just come in. What's… what's wrong?
DANIEL 1	Everything.
NORA 1	That's not like you.
DANIEL 1	Yeah. Yeah. It's not like me but… I had a doctor's appointment this morning.
NORA 1	What?
DANIEL 1	Went to the doctor with a pain in my ribs I couldn't shift. Yeah? Just a pain I couldn't… so eventually I went to the doctor's.
NORA 1	Why didn't you say anything?

DANIEL 1	Because that's not like me.
NORA 1	You should have said something.
DANIEL 1	But it's not like me. And actually, I didn't want to tell you, but it seems I could barely step six inches into your home without it spilling out.
	They found something in my lungs.
	I thought – it being me, it would be nothing. I've had plenty to deal with already and this is just another thing I would deal with, but I got results back this morning... it's aggressive. The growth, the treatment, it's all very... aggressive is the word they kept using. Didn't your dad have /
NORA 1	Yeah. Lung cancer.
DANIEL 1	Nice guy? Your old man?
NORA 1	I mean he wasn't... perfect. Let me get Tommy /
DANIEL 1	No. I'd rather he didn't know.
NORA 1	But you've told me?
DANIEL 1	I'd like to keep it private.
NORA 1	Then why tell me?
DANIEL 1	Because I had to tell someone. Because it's a lot... you know... it's a lot. It's a lot to imagine being forgotten.
NORA 1	You won't be forgotten.
DANIEL 1	There isn't much to remember me by... I thought about a will. Drafting a will but then I realised I wouldn't have anybody to leave anything too. Not that there is much to leave. My mother's jewellery, maybe, there is some money in that. Maybe, I should sell it... leave

	all my money to charity. Do one last good thing. Or have one big last party. A real big piss-up.
NORA 1	You think it could be worth something?
DANIEL 1	I imagine it is worth something. Aquamarine. Isn't that what they call it? Little stones in her ring, like water.
	Silence.
NORA 1	What if…
DANIEL 1	What?
NORA 1	No, it's just…
DANIEL 1	Hey, now. I've had a good shot at living, now it's a chance to try the alternative.
NORA 1	Danny.
DANIEL 1	And if you think I'm not going to that party tomorrow – you're wrong. I'm going to drink and dance and sing and shout until… until I can't.
NORA 1	Then I'll dance with you… for you. Would you like that?
DANIEL 1	Any guy likes to be danced for.
NORA 1	Then I'd like to dance for you.
DANIEL 1	And what should I do for you?
	Silence. NORA *pulls up her dress to reveal her underwear.*
NORA 1	Look at these stockings. I'm going to be wearing these… I'm just trying them on while Christine fixes my dress.
	Tomorrow, only the feet will be seen… but I thought I'd try them on.
	Do you want to feel them?

DANIEL 1	Nora, I…
NORA 1	I'm asking if you want to feel them.
DANIEL 1	Have you been drinking?
NORA 1	No. It's just cheap perfume. Go on.
DANIEL 1	No. Nora it's…
NORA 2	You can do it.
NORA 3	I know you want to.
DANIEL 1	But what if…
NORA 3	I do not mind.
DANIEL 1	Your eyes are glassy.
NORA 2	It's just the light.
NORA 1	I'm saying it's alright.
NORA 3	I'm giving you my permission.
DANIEL 1	Then I would like to touch you… very much.
NORA (*all*)	After all, it's just… skin.
NORA 1	Just skin.

He rubs his hand down her leg. His eyes close. She is steely with a sense that she is fighting back tears. She talks as he rubs.

Suppose I were to ask you… for something…

DANIEL 1	Anything. Ask me, anything.
NORA 1	Are you sure?
DANIEL 1	Tell me what you want.

His hand reaches her feet.

NORA 1	Again.
DANIEL 1	No. Nora it's…

NORA 2	You can do it.
NORA 3	I know you want to.
DANIEL 1	But what if…
NORA 3	I do not mind.
DANIEL 1	Your eyes are glassy.
NORA 2	It's just the light.
NORA 1	I'm saying it's alright.
NORA 3	I'm giving you my permission.
DANIEL 1	Then I would like to touch you… very much.
NORA (*all*)	After all, it's just… skin.
NORA 1	Just skin.

He rubs his hand down her leg. His eyes close. She is steely with a sense that she is fighting back tears. His hand reaches her feet.

DANIEL 2	Thank you.
NORA 2	I need something, Dan.
DANIEL 2	Tell me. Tell me what you need and if I can, I will give it to you.
NORA 2	But, if it's too much you must /
DANIEL 2	You've no idea, do you?
NORA 2	What?
DANIEL 2	I said to myself I would let you know before I… ever since I met you, I've had these feelings for you… not simple feelings either… not just wanting to touch you… not just that but wanting to… no, it's not that simple, because… I love you, Nora. I think I've always loved you.
NORA 2	Love?

DANIEL 2	Don't you know what it means to want something? Secretly?
NORA 2	I can imagine.
DANIEL 2	Have I spoilt everything?
NORA 2	No. No. I'm just... surprised.
DANIEL 2	I didn't mean to shock you.
NORA 2	No, it's...
DANIEL 2	What is it you wanted? Because I'd like to... if I can... help.
	Silence.
NORA 2	No. Dan. It wasn't anything important. You've got enough to deal with. It was silly of me to... I think Tom is smoking outside.
DANIEL 2	Then I'll go join him. Though I suppose I should think about stopping... if there is a point to that.
NORA 2	Don't you have hope?
DANIEL 2	No. Hope, can be so cruel. Don't you think?
	He goes to leave.
NORA 2	Dan? I'm sorry.
DANIEL 2	For what?
	You are worth love, Nora. I suddenly got a sense you don't think that. You are worth love.
	DANIEL *leaves.*
NORA 1	And as her breath is pulled out of her.
NORA 2	In the distance she can hear the river.
NORA 3	Calling to her. Calming her.
NORA 1	And she wonders – if this is everything.

NORA 2	Just everything.
NORA 3	And there is nothing more.
	A knock on the door. NORA *opens it – it's* NATHAN.
	Nathan.
	He just stands there, unable to talk.
	Nathan.
NATHAN 3	Structural changes? Structural changes. You cannot just take a man's job. Tell him he has just four weeks left at work. Four weeks' worth of pay and... I got the message not even an hour ago. Did you even try to stop him?
NORA 3	Please know, I tried my /
NATHAN 3	And you do not have money either – do you?
NORA 1	And she has no reply.
NORA 2	She has nothing to offer him.
NORA 3	To this man who is so willing to ruin everything.
NATHAN 3	All I want is a life worth living. All I want is my children to be safe and secure in their future.
NORA 1	But she couldn't, and she can't.
NORA 2	She couldn't, and she can't control him.
NORA 3	She couldn't, and she can't control any of them.
NATHAN 3	But your husband has taken that from me, so I am taking everything from you. Here is the proof. With a letter, detailing everything you have done. I will send one to the police and here is a copy for your husband.

NATHAN *pulls out a letter.*

NORA 3	I will not give it to him.
NORA 2	I'll rip the telephone out the wall.
NORA 1	I'll drown his phone.
NATHAN 3	You cannot stop me. Because all I would do is find another way.
NORA 3	He will see your name on the letter and hunt you down.
NATHAN 3	The letter is anonymous, there is no evidence it is me.
NORA 3	And if I destroy it?
NATHAN 3	Then he will find out from the police turning up at your door. So, I suppose this letter is an opportunity to have the conversation on your own terms. Before you cannot.
NORA 3	You talk like it is an act of charity. You are deluded.
NATHAN 3	Probably.
	And tomorrow. Tomorrow. I shall send the same letter to the police with the evidence of what you have done. Because at least that gives you a chance to kiss your children goodbye. I am giving you that.
NORA 1	If I go to prison, I'll die. Nathan.
NORA 2	It will kill me.
NORA 3	It will tear me in two.
NATHAN 3	My old man used to say debt is a form of death, suppose he is right.
	Good luck, Nora. Good luck to us all.

NATHAN *places the letter down and leaves.* NORA *watches it.*

NORA 1   And out of nowhere, a woman has a desperate need to be held by her dad. A dad who died years ago. But the memory and the need of his arms are so clear in her mind it almost knocks her to her knees. But it doesn't, she just stands tracing a sliver of a scar from last Christmas. A Christmas she could barely afford. A Christmas that pushed her to the red line of no return. A Christmas full of tantrums and tired kids and broken toys and too much to drink and not enough money, and as she stood washing her wine glass. One of the few thin and delicate things in her home. And just as she went to rinse it, she held it a little too tight and it broke in her hand and a tiny piece of glass pierced her palm. The washing-up water slowly turned red. All slow motion and sadness and she watched the foam flicker with bright-red bubbles. She was left with a cut in the shape of a 'C'. 'C' for Christmas she thinks. 'C' for children. 'C' for careful. 'C' for cunt. 'C' for can't. 'C' for can't do this. 'C' for can't do this any more. 'C' for can't breathe. 'C' for can't breathe. 'C' for I can't breathe any more. 'C' for I can't breathe any more. 'C' for...

CHRISTINE *enters.*

Christine?

CHRISTINE 1   Done. Your dress is as good as new. What's wrong? You look like you've seen a ghost.

NORA 1   Nathan.

CHRISTINE 1   What about him?

NORA 1	That money? He knows how I got it and is blackmailing me, because I...
NORA 3	I have done something terrible, Christine. And he knows what.
NORA 2	Nathan is threatening to tell the police what I have done.
NORA 1	Fraud. Christine. I am a...
CHRISTINE 1	What?
NORA (*all*)	A thief.
NORA 2	I want you to be my witness.
CHRISTINE 2	To what?
NORA 2	If I should lose my mind and they try to blame Thomas. Tell them it was my fault.
NORA 3	I am the one who poisoned this family.
NORA 1	I brought this fucking shit into this house.
CHRISTINE 2	What are you saying?
NORA 2	I did this all by myself.
NORA 1	I have wrecked this family.
NORA 3	Destroyed everything.
CHRISTINE 1	Nora. Please let me help.
CHRISTINE 2	Nora, calm yourself.
CHRISTINE 3	Nora, there is one thing I can do.
CHRISTINE (*all*)	I'll go and talk to Nathan.
NORA (*all*)	No, Christine, don't!
CHRISTINE (*all*)	Let me try and help.
NORA (*all*)	He'll only hurt you too.
CHRISTINE (*all*)	Trust me. Nora. He won't hurt me.

NORA 2	What do you mean?
NORA 1	Christine? Why wouldn't he hurt you?
NORA 3	He only lives around the corner – I think. I don't know.
THOMAS (*all*)	(*Offstage.*) Nora!
NORA 1	Don't come in!
NORA 2	I'm trying on my dress!
NORA 3	I am not ready.
THOMAS (*all*)	(*Offstage.*) In the living room?
NORA 1	Don't come in!
NORA 3	Please, Thomas. Give me a minute.
NORA 2	Wait! The house with the yellow door. He told me that... there is only one house with a yellow door... please be quick.
THOMAS (*all*)	(*Offstage.*) Nora?
CHRISTINE 3	I promise, Nora. I'll do my very best. I'll run as fast as I can.

NORA *grabs on to* CHRISTINE.

NORA 2	Thank you. Thank you. Thank you.
CHRISTINE 2	Of course, my – sweetheart.
NORA 2	Christine, I just...

NORA *kisses* CHRISTINE, *on the lips, hard.* NORA *is shocked at her own actions and lets go.*

I'm sorry. I'm so... sorry.

CHRISTINE 2	No.
THOMAS 2	(*Offstage.*) Nora?

The two women are held in a moment.

(*Offstage.*) I'm waiting...

CHRISTINE 2	My dearest Nora.
NORA 2	Christine… I…
CHRISTINE 2	I'll be as quick as I can.
	CHRISTINE *exits*. THOMAS *enters*.
THOMAS 2	I thought you were changing?
NORA 2	I was… changing out of it. You can't see me in my dress before tomorrow. Isn't that bad luck? Where is Daniel?
THOMAS 2	He stepped outside the back door to say hello to the children. Am I leaving a trail of my papers?
	THOMAS *picks up* NATHAN's *letter*.
NORA 2	No! Please. Tom.
THOMAS 2	Endless paperwork.
	THOMAS *keeps a hold of the letter and walks toward the files he left earlier*.
	I should put this all away in the office. Remember what happened last time the children got a hold of my work? Paper aeroplanes, the lot of it.
NORA 2	No. You can't leave.
	She suddenly kisses him very hard. She tries to reach for the letter and fails.
THOMAS 3	Such force. Where did that come from?
NORA 3	I… I… think that is for me?
THOMAS 3	With my name on it?
	THOMAS *goes to open it*. NORA *kisses him again. She tries to reach for the letter and fails*.
THOMAS 1	Nora.

NORA 1   Put down your work. Put down your work and… let me touch you… let me… show you how good I can make you feel.

                NORA *kisses* THOMAS, *again.*

THOMAS 1   Alright. Alright I… just let me put this work away.

                THOMAS *picks up the files. He still has the letter.*

NORA 1   No. Just stay with me.

THOMAS 1   Nora.

NORA 1   Come on.

THOMAS 1   Nora.

NORA 1   Just stay with me.

THOMAS 1   Nora! Stop it! You're pissing me off. Just let me put these away with everything else, before the kids fuck up another important document.

                THOMAS *leaves.*

NORA 1   And just like that. He walks out the room with the letter in his hand.

NORA 3   And he goes to his desk, places the papers in a drawer and locks it.

NORA 2   And she can barely watch because she doesn't know where he keeps the key.

NORA 3   And she tries to remember a time when she wasn't frightened by his fury.

NORA 1   But she can't, and she is paralysed by panic.

NORA (*all*)   Oh my god.

                THOMAS *enters.*

THOMAS 2	Look. Before I sit down to work, I just wanted to say – I'm sorry, I didn't mean to lose my temper, but this time of year is just /
NORA 2	Where do you keep the key for your desk?
THOMAS 2	What? Why? There is nothing in there for /
NORA 2	You never told me, and you should tell me. Please.
THOMAS 2	I don't have time for this nonsense, Nora. I have to work /
NORA (all)	No. Stay out of the office.
THOMAS 2	Why? What do you want?
NORA 2	I want us... I want us to be together like it is the last time we will be together.
THOMAS 2	That is a little dramatic.
NORA 1	No, I just want. I want to keep you close.
NORA 3	I want you to be here with me.
NORA 2	Don't step another foot into your office. Because we should... why don't we...
NORA (all)	Dance.
NORA 1	Here. I'll put some music on.
NORA 3	We can practise for the party.
NORA 1	Come on! It will be fun!
THOMAS (all)	Nora.
NORA 2	Here. I'll put some music on.
NORA 1	We can practise for the party.
NORA 3	Come on! It will be fun!
NORA 2	Just be with me.
NORA 1	Here.

NORA 3	With me.
NORA (*all*)	Like it's the last time.
THOMAS (*all*)	Fine.
NORA (*all*)	So. Dance with me.

The music begins to play. NORA *takes* THOMAS *in her arms.*

Right here.

NORA 2	Put your arms there.
NORA 3	Watch my feet.
THOMAS (*all*)	Nora.

They begin to dance.

NORA 1	Right here.
NORA 2	Put your arms there.
NORA 3	Watch my feet.
THOMAS (*all*)	Nora.

The dance gets quicker.

NORA 1	Right here.
NORA 2	Put your arms there.
NORA 3	Watch my feet.
THOMAS (*all*)	Nora. Slower!

And quicker. Finally, THOMAS *drops his hands and backs off.*

Nora!

THOMAS 1	Not so fast. You dance like a wild woman. I can't keep up.
NORA (*all*)	Fine! Then I'll dance with myself if I have to.
THOMAS 1	Fine.

NORA 1	Watch me.
	NORA *begins to dance by herself – increasingly violently.* THOMAS *watches. She dances and dances, lost in the moment. There is something wild and free about her movements.* THOMAS *gets lost in the watching. Until* CHRISTINE *enters.*
	Christine!
CHRISTINE 1	What a show.
THOMAS 1	Dancing like a madwoman. I swear we haven't had a drink.
NORA 1	Tommy. Promise me, you'll dance with me tomorrow until the end of the night?
THOMAS 1	Do you plan on dancing like that?
NORA 1	Just say you'll dance with me.
THOMAS 1	Sure. Okay… how about a drink? Christine? It's 6 p.m. somewhere.
CHRISTINE 1	Yeah, I'll take a drink of something.
NORA 1	I say we'll drink until dawn – or death – whatever should happen first.
THOMAS 1	You've got a taste for the dramatic today.
	DANIEL *enters.*
DANIEL 1	Those kids are balls of energy. I don't know how you do it.
NORA 1	But you're so good with them.
THOMAS 1	It's true. You'll be a good dad, one day. A drink?
DANIEL 1	I can't think of a reason why not.
THOMAS 1	Nora – bring the kids in, will you? They've spent all afternoon out there, people will think they are feral, and you know how people like to talk.

NORA 1   Okay, I'll get them. Just give me a minute to catch my breath.

THOMAS and DANIEL leave.

CHRISTINE 2   Nora. I can't find Nathan. No one is home. Not him. Not his children. But I left him a note asking to speak with him. Maybe, there is still time to fix all this.

NORA 2   I think it would take a miracle.

CHRISTINE 2   In the note, I begged him to think of your children. To think of /

NORA 2   You know what, Christine?

CHRISTINE 2   What?

NORA 2   I wish I could undo my children. I couldn't say it earlier but now I feel free to say anything. I wish they had never been born to me. I wish they had never grown inside of me. I wish this house was empty, as if they had never existed. I wish a doctor had ripped them out of me. A pill had destroyed them before they had ever been destined to be.

Because they deserve better than me.

CHRISTINE 2   Oh, Nora.

NORA 2   But my life is just a few years too late... nothing at all, really. How different life could have been.

NORA steps towards CHRISTINE. They look at each other.

And I have these feelings. For you. Complicated... feelings. Do you... do you?

CHRISTINE 2   Yes. It's true. I have feelings for you too. Feelings beyond friendship.

NORA 2   But what are we... what are we meant to do with these feelings?

CHRISTINE 2	Well. When we talked earlier you to seemed to warm to the idea that men might cohabit or that /
NORA 2	But isn't it different for men? Everything always seems so different for men.
CHRISTINE 2	But isn't it for once good that we are invisible? That people care less about us? We can hide in plain sight. Plus, the world is changing.
NORA 2	But not quick enough.
CHRISTINE 2	You are choosing to /
NORA 2	What choice does someone like me have?
CHRISTINE 2	But what... what if love... what if I love you.
	Silence.
NORA 2	But what if love is not enough?
	What if – sometimes – love is not enough.
	Silence. THOMAS *enters.*
THOMAS 2	You never said what you wanted to drink, Christine.
CHRISTINE 2	You know – I think I will leave. I'd hate to get in the way.
NORA 2	You aren't in the way.
	NORA *reaches out and grabs* CHRISTINE*'s hand.*
	Stay.
	Silence.
THOMAS 3	Do I need to pour another glass or not?
NORA 3	Please stay.
	Silence.

CHRISTINE 3	No. I am afraid, I cannot. Not this lifetime.
THOMAS 3	How many lifetimes do you plan on having, Christine?
CHRISTINE 3	I should hope the next one is rather simpler than this.
THOMAS 3	The world is getting better by the day.
CHRISTINE 3	Maybe for you.
NORA 3	Christine?
CHRISTINE 3	You are at the party tomorrow?

NORA *nods*.

Then... shall I sit with the children while you are out? Then I can see you before and after the party to make sure, I mean... to see you in your dress.

THOMAS 3	What a kind offer, but we could not possibly /
CHRISTINE 3	No. I would like to be here. I did just fix the dress – I would like to see it.
THOMAS 3	Then... we shall see you tomorrow.
CHRISTINE 3	Wonderful. Enjoy your drink.
NORA 3	Thank you. And be careful, it gets dark so early this time of year.
CHRISTINE 3	I think there is still a little light left. And if you should need me, I am only the other side of the river, opposite a statue of... well, of some man who did something.
THOMAS 3	He is actually /
CHRISTINE 3	I shall see you tomorrow.
THOMAS 3	Until tomorrow.
NORA 3	Thank you.

CHRISTINE *leaves.*

THOMAS 3   You know, she reminds me of someone, but I cannot place her... will you come into the kitchen? I thought you could make some hot chocolate for the children. I think they'd like that, would they not?

NORA 3   Yes, I suppose they would.

THOMAS 3   Call them in. And then join us.

THOMAS *leaves.* NORA *goes to the door.*

NORA (*all*)   Children. It's time to come in. It's getting dark.

NORA 1   And as she watches her children run in, for a moment she imagines herself running into the river until her body bashes against the bedrock. Submerging herself. In the cold and calm.

NORA 2   She imagines taking deep breaths of cold water. Rinsing out her ribs until her body becomes bleached and barren.

NORA 3   Washing off the weight and waste of all this life. And there is so much life to live. And the opposite might be a relief. What she realises now, so sharply, so clearly, is that death might be a relief.

THOMAS 2   (*Offstage.*) Songbird?

THOMAS (*all*)   (*Offstage.*) We're waiting.

NORA (*all*)   Your songbird is right here.

DAY THREE

NORA 1	It's dawn and she lies awake. Watching the sun attempting to shine through the curtains.
NORA 2	And she hasn't slept, and she hasn't moved. Pinned in place.
NORA 3	And when she hears her children begin to stir, she exhales for the first time in hours.
NORA 1	She spends the day in a daze. Automated actions of mothering and managing and making sure. A whole lifetime spent – making sure. And from the outside there is no discernible difference to this day in December.
NORA 2	From the outside everything appears to be fine. It's breakfast then lunch then dinner and the children play and laugh and cry and it's a day like any other day.
NORA 3	And suddenly it's 8 p.m., again, and she tucks her children into bed and kisses them on their foreheads. And they smell of sunshine and soap and hope. Her children smell of hope.
NORA 2	And her husband calls her and tells her they must leave. A party is waiting for them. And she kisses each of her children on their foreheads.
NORA 1	And it takes all her strength not to cry. It takes all her strength to stay upright. And she whispers to them.

NORA (*all*)	Goodnight, my sweethearts. I love you. I love you so much, I can barely breathe.

The front door creaks open – it's NATHAN.

NATHAN 2	Christine?
CHRISTINE 2	Nathan?
NATHAN 2	They're out?
CHRISTINE 2	Tom and Nora are at a party. I offered to look after their children.
NATHAN 2	You look at home in their living room.
CHRISTINE 2	It's just a living room, like any other. Please come in. Don't stand in the doorway like that. Please.

NATHAN *hesitates. Enters.*

NATHAN 2	I got the note you left. I went to where you said you were staying but they said you were here and… it's been a while.
CHRISTINE 2	Years. It's been years.
NATHAN 2	How was his money?
CHRISTINE 2	Don't be like that.
NATHAN 2	Does Nora know about us? Know how we used to be together?
CHRISTINE 2	No. But a lot has changed since then.
NATHAN 2	She doesn't know how you chose a nice house over love?
CHRISTINE 2	It's not that simple.
NATHAN 2	It's not much more complicated. Sometimes I think about how different I might have been if we'd stayed together… But look… here you are… years after breaking my heart, you're back to take my job.

CHRISTINE 2   I didn't know it was your job. And trust me, my life has not been that simple since we last saw each other. And it's true, Nathan. All those years ago, I left you for a man who had money. I wanted a safe and secure future – something that you couldn't provide.

NATHAN 2   Then why aren't you still with him?

CHRISTINE 2   Because the world has changed and back then I didn't know what I really wanted. I thought I had no choice back then.

NATHAN 2   There is always a choice.

CHRISTINE 2   No, there isn't.

NATHAN 2   So. What do you want? Are you about to propose a second chance? A rekindling? Because I don't think now is the time for romance.

CHRISTINE 2   No. I am not proposing a romance. There is a lot to tell you but there isn't time… I know what you have done, what you've done to Nora. But despite that I still care for you. And so, I suppose what I am proposing is that you are not this man. This blackmailing, mean, malicious man.

NATHAN 2   Maybe I have become that man.

CHRISTINE 2   No. I know you. I know you so well, Nathan McKinnon. The years do not change that you are a good man who has faced difficult times.

NATHAN 2   Difficult times? I am broken, Christine. My heart, my everything is smashed to pieces. And I thought it was mended by meeting my wife but it seems there are a thousand ways for a person to break.

CHRISTINE 2   I understand that you miss having someone.

NATHAN 2	No. I don't miss it. I crave it.
CHRISTINE 2	Then let me help you.
NATHAN 2	But Christine…
CHRISTINE 2	Maybe the two of us – shipwrecked survivors – can find a way. To be friends, maybe. I am not talking romance, you understand but… Please. Be the man better than what has happened to him.
	CHRISTINE *reaches out and holds* NATHAN. NATHAN *is reluctant but finally gives way to the warmth of her arms.*
NATHAN 2	It has been years since I have been held.
CHRISTINE (*all*)	I know.
NATHAN 2	You are softening me to help your friend.
CHRISTINE 2	Or maybe I simply see another friend who I hurt, many years ago. Who I wish to help heal.
NATHAN 2	But I've done terrible things. Unforgivable things.
CHRISTINE (*all*)	I know.
NATHAN 2	Then why are you being so kind to me? It's been years since…
CHRISTINE 2	Shouldn't people look after one another during terrible times like this? Nathan McKinnon – you can choose to be a good man.
CHRISTINE 1	Please, Nathan. Don't do this. This isn't you.
CHRISTINE 3	As you said yourself – there is always a choice.
NATHAN 3	But, Christine… I cannot undo what I have done. There is no way for me to take back the letter.

CHRISTINE 1	Then maybe we should just let them read it. Because if it's love… well, that has to mean something. Doesn't it?
NATHAN 1	I've no idea.
	I'm sorry… for the things I've done.
CHRISTINE 3	I am too. It seems we have both lived a million lives and I would like to try and help you. We can meet? When all this has passed? Take the time to see the truth in each other.
NATHAN 3	Yes. I would like that. And thank you.
CHRISTINE (*all*)	For what?
NATHAN 2	You helped me feel less alone. Which is the greatest gift.
	Silence.
CHRISTINE 2	I think I hear people outside. Quickly out the back, just in case. Goodnight, Nathan.
NATHAN 2	Goodnight, Christine… and… goodnight.
	NATHAN *slips out the back door. We hear voices outside.* NORA *and* THOMAS *return to the sitting room. Taking off their jackets – they haven't noticed* CHRISTINE.
THOMAS 1	Fucking hell, could you have walked slower?
NORA 1	I wasn't finished dancing.
THOMAS 1	Yeah. Dancing like a madwoman.
NORA 1	I was having fun.
THOMAS 1	Is that what you'd call it?
NORA 1	I just wanted one last dance.
THOMAS 1	Well, maybe I wanted to come home to dance.

NORA 1	Well, maybe I didn't.
	NORA *suddenly spots* CHRISTINE *in the corner of the room.*
	Christine.
CHRISTINE 1	You had a good night?
THOMAS 1	The best. How were the kids?
CHRISTINE 1	They've just been sleeping since you left. You look great, Nora.
THOMAS 1	Isn't she the prettiest thing you've ever seen? Beautiful. Stubborn too. Her pretty little heart is stubborn.
NORA 1	You should have let me dance longer.
THOMAS 1	You made quite an exit, I had to drag you away from dancing. During which I've worked up a thirst and I need a nightcap.
NORA 1	And I'll have one!
THOMAS 1	A whisky? More like water for you, Nora Helmer.
	THOMAS *exits.*
CHRISTINE 1	I spoke to Nathan.
NORA 1	And?
CHRISTINE 1	He won't bother you again. I promise.
NORA 1	But Tommy still has that letter locked away and I'm still... fucked.
CHRISTINE 1	What if you told him what you did?
NORA 1	Why?
CHRISTINE 1	I know it will be hard but – do you want to live with all these lies?
NORA 1	But it will destroy him.

CHRISTINE 1	But if he loves you, Nora. He has to understand, what you did, you did for love.
	THOMAS *walks in, interrupting the moment.*
THOMAS 1	I love this time of year. It feels like you are just given constant reasons to drink.
CHRISTINE 1	I should go. Goodnight, Nora.
NORA 1	Goodnight, Christine.
THOMAS 1	And a merry Christmas!
	CHRISTINE *takes one last look at* NORA.
CHRISTINE 1	Merry Christmas.
	She leaves.
THOMAS 2	You look tired.
NORA 2	I am tired.
	Silence.
	Stop looking at me like that.
THOMAS 2	I can look at my little prize however I'd like to.
NORA 2	Don't say that.
THOMAS 2	It is just... you are the most beautiful thing.
NORA 2	You barely spoke to me all night.
THOMAS 2	Because I like to watch you. I like to pretend you are my secret. I like to pretend that I am taking you home for the first time. That I will be alone with you for the first time. And you're standing there – beautiful and trembling.
	THOMAS *moves towards* NORA.
NORA 2	What is beautiful about a woman trembling?

THOMAS 2	Trembling with lust – not trepidation.
	He starts to kiss her neck.
NORA 2	How can you tell the difference?
	THOMAS *puts his hand on her leg, moves it up her thigh.*
	Tom.
THOMAS 2	I cannot bear to take my lips off your skin.
NORA 2	Tom.
THOMAS 2	Can you feel how much I want you?
	THOMAS *places her hand on his groin. She snaps it away.*
NORA 2	I'm not in the mood.
THOMAS 2	But I'm your husband.
NORA 2	And I'm your wife and I'm not in the mood.
THOMAS 2	I have always managed to get you in the mood once we've started.
	THOMAS *grabs at her clothes.*
NORA 2	Stop it. You're drunk.
THOMAS 2	I'd like to see some of that skin…
NORA 2	Stop it.
THOMAS 2	Come here!
	A knock at the door. THOMAS *drops his hands.*
	Oh, what now.
	NORA *opens the door to* DANIEL. *He enters.*
NORA 3	Daniel.
DANIEL 3	Hello, dear Helmers.

THOMAS 3	It's not like you to call at night.
DANIEL 3	I am not interrupting, am I? I saw your light was on and /
NORA 3	I am quite glad you are here.
DANIEL 3	You both looked so happy tonight and here you are in your happy home.
THOMAS 3	You looked rather happy yourself tonight.
DANIEL 3	And why wouldn't I? Why shouldn't one make the most of this world? As much as one can, and for as long as one can... also the wine was excellent.
THOMAS 3	I hope my head does not regret it tomorrow.
DANIEL 3	You never get anything in this life without paying for it.
NORA 3	That is the truth.
THOMAS 3	And what would you know about paying for anything? Silly girl. A drink? Daniel? My skylark can fetch you one?
DANIEL 3	No, no. I shall simply ask what I came for – a cigar. I have left mine at home and I wished to enjoy one on my walk. There is nothing quite like smoking while it is snowing.
NORA 3	But is it wise for you to smoke? When... you have been feeling so tired.
THOMAS 3	A man can do as he wishes, Nora. And of course, my friend. Anything.
	THOMAS *gets a cigar and cuts it.*
NORA 3	How are you feeling?
DANIEL 3	You know, I am thinking of taking a trip. I am finding this bad weather rather relentless, time for a change, maybe.

NORA 3	But I will miss you. Ever such a lot.
DANIEL 3	And I will miss you. Ever such a lot.
THOMAS 3	Do not forget some matches, here take mine.
	THOMAS *hands a cigar and a box of matches to* DANIEL.
DANIEL 3	Thank you.
THOMAS 3	Goodnight. Enjoy the snow.
NORA 3	Wrap up warm, Daniel. It is going to be a cold night.
DANIEL 3	Goodnight. Thank you for the light. Such light.
	DANIEL *leaves*.
THOMAS 1	He has been drinking. It makes him so, far away.
NORA 1	And he will only get further away.
THOMAS 1	It's a little late for riddles.
NORA 1	He is ill. Really ill.
THOMAS 1	What?
NORA 1	Cancer. Tommy.
THOMAS 1	What? I should go and /
NORA 1	No. He wanted me to keep it a secret, but tonight I don't believe in secrets, any more.
THOMAS 1	Why didn't he tell me? Lie to me like this.
NORA 1	Because he wants your friendship to be – happy. And sometimes, there is a difference between happiness and truth.
THOMAS 3	Such news... come here. Come here.
	THOMAS *suddenly grabs* NORA.

I never want to let go of you. The thought of losing you my songbird… is too much. The thought that I would let a delicate creature like you, be hurt. I mean after one evening of drinking wine and you are already unsteady. I shall protect us both, from anything, everything.

NORA 3   I am not unsteady.

THOMAS 3   Oh. I know you better than you know yourself. I know what is best for you. My prized possession. My lovely little skylark.

                NORA *pushes him away.*

                Nora, please. I am vowing to protect you.

NORA 2   Am I just a little ornamental bird to you? Just a possession?

THOMAS 2   It's just a word.

NORA 2   Words can be powerful.

THOMAS 2   Oh, please. What would you know about the power of words?

                Silence.

NORA 2   There was a letter, one you locked away with your files. I suddenly thought it could be something urgent.

THOMAS 2   It can wait until the morning.

NORA 2   No. I don't think it can.

THOMAS 2   There is no such thing as urgent at Christmas.

NORA 2   Then a gift. Maybe? A little Christmas gift. I'd hate to miss something pretty to put on the mantelpiece. Please. For me. For silly old me.

THOMAS 2	Fine. I shall go hunt it out.
NORA 2	Thank you.
THOMAS 2	You really are very ridiculous.
NORA 2	Oh, I know. I am utterly ridiculous.
	THOMAS *kisses her on the forehead and leaves.* NORA *is left.*
NORA 3	My skeleton.
NORA 1	My ribcage.
NORA 2	My heart.
NORA 3	Blood and bile and body and /
NORA 2	Polluted and poisoned /
NORA 1	From milk into madness.
NORA 3	There is just so much life to live.
NORA (*all*)	Too much.
NORA 2	Must silence these thoughts.
NORA 1	Must drown it out.
NORA 3	Flood it out.
NORA 1	Must silence these thoughts.
NORA 3	Must drown it out.
NORA 2	Flood it out.
NORA 3	Must silence these thoughts.
NORA 2	Must drown it out.
NORA 1	Flood it out.
NORA 3	I'll run into the river.
NORA 2	Until I brush up against the bedrock.
NORA 1	And I breathe only cold water.
NORA (*all*)	I'll drown myself.

NORA 1   Goodbye. My sweethearts.

NORA 2   Goodbye.

NORA 3   Goodbye.

NORA 1   Goodbye. Goodbye. Goodbye. Goodbye.
                Good... good.

                NORA *takes a deep breath, turns to leave.*
                THOMAS *walks in clutching* NATHAN'*s*
                letter.

THOMAS 1   What the fuck is this? Nora? This letter?
                Is this true? What you, how you got that
                money? Is this true?

                NORA *nods.*

                What?

NORA 1   Yes. It's true.

THOMAS 1   And do you know who sent it? Who sent
                this letter? Who... oh my god.

NORA 1   I was trying to save you.

THOMAS 1   Save me? This is your way of saving me?
                By lying to me? About all this. All this
                borrowed money. You said it was your dad's
                but you... it was illegal what you... Nora.
                What the fuck were you thinking? If anyone
                else found out – it's illegal, Nora. This is
                police, this is prison, what the fuck were
                you thinking? And the kids? I left you to
                look after my kids and... and we don't have
                fucking anything and still you managed to
                fuck it up more. You fucked everything up,
                you stupid little bitch. Because who else
                knows? Who else, look at me. Fucking
                looking at me. I said who else knows?

                THOMAS *goes to grab* NORA, *but she*
                keeps moving away.

	Look at me. I said look at me. I said look at me. I said look at me.
	THOMAS *grabs on to* NORA, *lifts his hand to backhand her. The sudden cry of a child from another room. It stops* THOMAS *instantly, he lets go of her. Drops his hand.*
NORA 1	I should /
THOMAS 1	No. Stay here.
	She'll settle.
	The crying stops. A long silence.
	Why, Nora. Why did you /
NORA 1	When you got sick and you weren't earning, I had to find a way to pay for everything, because otherwise we would have lost it. We were on the edge of losing everything and I brought us back. I did that. And I did it for love. I risked it all for... love.
THOMAS 1	Why didn't you just tell me?
NORA 1	Because I was scared.
NORA 2	I was scared of you.
NORA 3	Because I am scared of everything.
	Long silence.
NORA 1	And his mobile beeps with a message.
NORA 2	The house phone rings.
NORA 3	A telegram delivered.
THOMAS 1	Oh, what now.
	THOMAS *goes to receive the message.*
NORA 1	Silence and stillness surrounds and drowns her.
NORA 3	To think of waves.

NORA 2	And wounds.
NORA 1	And washing away.
	For the first time the NORAS suddenly acknowledge each other.
NORA (*all*)	This is it.
NORA 2	This is really it.
NORA 1	I'm sorry.
NORA 3	But maybe there was never any choice.
NORA 2	Maybe this really is everything.
NORA 1	But I…
NORA 3	I know. I know.
	Silence. THOMAS *enters. The* NORAS *become unnoticeable to each other again.*
NORA 2	What was it?
	THOMAS *hesitates.*
THOMAS 2	Nathan. It was Nathan McKinnon… He was the one who was going to blackmail you?
NORA 2	What did he say?
THOMAS 2	That he will no longer notify the police or anyone of any wrongdoing. If we quietly pay back your debt he will destroy any evidence of any wrongdoing.
	He will destroy… we are free.
NORA 2	But how? Why?
THOMAS 2	He said he wished to be a better man. He said…
	Silence.
	We are free.

NORA (*all*)	I am free.
THOMAS 2	And I am saved. We are both... saved.

THOMAS *goes to her, she moves away.*

I am sorry for what I said... I was angry. I'm sorry for... oh, my skylark. This must have worried you.

You made a silly decision because you didn't know any better. I forgive you for what you did, and I am sorry for my angry words, but you must understand... I thought our world was crumbling around us. But now, I see what you did was for love. I forgive you.

NORA 2	It's amazing how quickly...

NORA *turns to leave.*

THOMAS 2	What? Where are you going?
NORA 2	To change.

NORA *steps in the room next door to get changed.*

THOMAS 2	Yes, you're right. Now is the time for calm. You must have been so frightened little songbird but don't worry... I shall make sure no harm is ever done to you. It will take time, Nora. To forget all this but tomorrow will be quite different. Do you ever think I could bring myself to disown you – no, to forgive you frees my heart. I have given you the gift of a second chance and that brings me joy. If you think about it, for the second time – it seems – I have made you a wife and a mother. Never be frightened again. Little songbird. Never again.

NORA *walks in. Dressed in her normal daytime clothes.*

THOMAS 3   You have changed?

NORA 3   I have changed.

THOMAS 3   You would be better to change into your
                nightclothes. Soon it will be time for some
                quiet.

NORA 3   I do not have time for quiet. When there is
                such a lot to say to you.

THOMAS 3   I do not understand.

NORA 3   No, it is I who has not understood you.
                Until this very evening. We have been
                married for years and does it not occur to
                you that this is the first time we have had
                a serious conversation?

THOMAS 3   Nonsense.

NORA 3   Exactly. We have spoken nothing but
                nonsense for all these years.

                You see you never understood me. First
                Father and now you.

THOMAS 3   Two men who loved you?

NORA 3   Two men who thought it fun to love me.
                I look back on it all and I realise everything
                is arranged the way you want it. I simply
                took over your taste or I pretended I did –
                I don't really know which. Now, I see I have
                actually been living as a pauper, from hand
                to mouth. I perform tricks for you and you
                gave me money and food because that is all
                you wanted from me. Maybe it is your fault
                that I have done nothing with my life? Or
                maybe it was Father's or maybe… or maybe
                it is my own.

THOMAS 3   You have not been happy?

NORA 3   I used to think I was… but what I see now
                is our home has been nothing but a
                playroom. I am a doll-wife.

THOMAS 3   Maybe, there is some truth in what you say.
                But, now you can learn to be another way.

NORA 3   Learn? You are trying to educate me in
                being a wife? How about teaching me to be
                a mother? You did say just moments ago
                that I was not fit to be a mother.

THOMAS 3   In a moment of crisis.

NORA 3   But the truth is – you are right. I am not fit
                to be with the children. If I am to learn to be
                a mother, first I must learn to be myself…
                by myself.

THOMAS 3   What?

NORA 3   I am leaving you.

THOMAS 3   You have lost your mind.

NORA 3   No. For the first time this lifetime I see it so
                clearly. I see it so clearly it would scare you.

THOMAS 3   I am scared, Nora. What you are saying…

NORA 3   I will take nothing but what is mine.

                NORA *looks around the room*.

                Which seems to be nothing at all.

THOMAS 3   Leave your husband? Your children? What
                will people say?

NORA 3   I cannot help what people will say.

THOMAS 3   It is monstrous for you to leave your
                children. Your most sacred duty.

NORA 3   A sacred duty? I have a duty equally sacred
                – a duty to myself.

THOMAS 3	First and foremost, you are a mother and a wife.
NORA 2	No.
NORA 1	No.
NORA 3	No.
	I believe that I am first and foremost a human being.
NORA (*all*)	Because my heart beats for me.
NORA 2	And not once have you asked for my opinion about our life together.
NORA 1	You've hurt me. You've done terrible things.
THOMAS 1	I am sorry if I have hurt you. I am so very... but if you walk – you'll have nothing. Nora. Your purse is empty. You have no idea of how the world works.
NORA (*all*)	Then I'd like to learn.
THOMAS 3	You don't love me?
	When did you stop?
NORA 1	This evening.
NORA (*all*)	I was waiting for a miracle.
NORA 1	I thought you might stand up for me.
NORA 3	I was waiting for you to see what this marriage really is and to take equal blame for it.
THOMAS 2	I would gladly work day and night for you, endure sorrow and hardship for your sake. But no man can be expected to sacrifice /
NORA 2	His honour? His pride? No, this man would not sacrifice it. When every day, thousands of women sacrifice their honour for men.

THOMAS 3	You think and talk like a child.
NORA 3	Maybe. But you think and talk like a man I have no interest in sharing my life with.
NORA 1	Take a look around. Is this what you want for us? For life? Take a fucking look around?
THOMAS (*all*)	But the children?
	Silence.
NORA 3	For the last few days I have done nothing but send the children outside to play. Employ a nanny, then they will have an adult who actually spends time with them.
NORA 2	There is so much about myself and my desires that I do not understand but wish to... and I won't subject the children to that. Their world is not ready for mine.
NORA 1	The kids' uniforms need washed before they go back to school after Christmas. Iron them too, won't you? I like them to look smart. The iron is kept under the sink. The steam setting is broken but... you'll make do. Just like I did.
THOMAS 1	But you are walking out of this house with nothing. No money. No family. You've no one but me. There is nowhere else for you. You'll freeze to death.
NORA 3	I will leave your ring.
NORA 2	I'll leave my keys.
NORA 1	I'll leave my phone... in it you'll find all the dates you'll need for all the kids' appointments and... look after them, won't you?
THOMAS 3	But where will you go?

NORA 3   You know, Thomas. I have never seen
                beyond this street, not in years. So, I think
                I will walk there and simply keep on
                walking because I want to see... I just want
                to see what could happen.

THOMAS 1   But you've got no friends. No family. No
                money. Bus stop around the corner... that's
                all you've got. So. Don't be stupid.

NORA 1   Oh, fuck me, do I feel stupid. I feel stupid
                for staying so fucking long. Because I think
                I hate you. I think I might actually hate you.

NORA 2   I love life. Thomas. I love life so much
                I could burst, and you took that from me.
                And how dare you take it. Because my life is
                not ridiculous. My life is worth something.

NORA 3   For weeks we have been raising toasts to the
                war ending, but it seems not all wars have
                ended, not all wars have battlefields.

THOMAS 3   This is not a war.

NORA 3   Then why are we both so wounded?

THOMAS 1   Nora? Please. I can change.

NORA 1   Then change.

                NORA *walks out the front door. The door
                closes.* THOMAS *disappears.*

NORA 3   And it's 1918. And she walks through the
                snow, quicker and quicker until she is
                almost running, until her face flushes red
                with the exertion, until she can't tell the
                difference between her tears and sweat. She
                runs until her front door is nothing but a dot.

NORA 2   And it's 1968. And she walks through the
                snow until she ends up on the doorstep
                where her friend is staying. She holds her

heart and hope in her hands as her knuckles knock the door. Her friend answers it in her nightdress and tears fill her eyes.

NORA 1   And it's 2018. And she walks through the snow until she reaches that bus stop, the one place she can shelter. And she stands under it, for the longest moments of her life. Tears dripping down her face, freezing as they fall. And she realises she has nowhere else to go.

NORA (*all*)   And tears fall down her face.

NORA 3   And she runs, and she runs, and she runs. Until she falls to the ground in exhilaration and exhaustion.

NORA 2   And she asks if she can stay the night. And she steps into her friend's home and into her arms that hold her.

NORA 1   And she knows there are no shelters near here. No community centres. No nothing. Not any more.

NORA (*all*)   And tears fall down her face.

NORA 3   And as she lays down in the snow, she knows that she would give up a lifetime of imprisonment, for fifteen minutes of free. And she lets the cold and the snow hold her like a hug, and she smiles, and she closes her eyes.

NORA 2   And as they close the front door, one hand slips into another. Neither of them thinks about anything else but the feeling of skin on skin. Two women, terrified, electrified by the possibility of this new existence.

NORA 1   And in the distance, she watches her husband walk towards her. Shaking and in shock, she knows that somehow, someway, someday, she'll be free.

NORA 3   It will be okay.

NORA 1   One day. Everything will be okay.

NORA 2   We can get through this. We always do.

NORA 1   Because what if this isn't everything.

NORA 2   What if this is just the beginning.

NORA 3   Because we won't stop.

NORA 2   We will never stop.

NORA 2   And I'm sorry we weren't quick enough.

NORA 1   To save you.

NORA 2   To help you save yourself.

NORA 3   Because I love you.

NORA 1   Because we are angry.

NORA 2   We are fucking furious.

NORA 3   And we are coming for your daughters, your sisters, your mothers, your lovers.

NORA 2   And we won't stop.

NORA 1   We'll never stop.

NORA 3   Until there is nothing left to do.

NORA 1   A woman.

NORA 2   A woman.

NORA 3   A woman walks /

NORA 1   A woman walks out of her home and she just...

The End.